# MODERN TANKS

&

# ARMOURED FIGHTING VEHICLES

**SIMON DUNSTAN**

**Airlife**
England

Copyright © 2002 Airlife Publishing Ltd

First published in the UK in 2002
by Airlife Publishing Ltd

**British Library Cataloguing-in-Publication Data**
A catalogue record for this book
is available from the British Library

ISBN 1 84037 190 0

Typeset by Echelon, Wimborne
Printed in Hong Kong

**Airlife Publishing Ltd**
101 Longden Road, Shrewsbury,
SY3 9EB, England
E-mail: sales@airlifebooks.com
Website: www.airlifebooks.com

# Contents

# 2S3 M1973
# and Gvozdika 2S1 M1974 SP Artillery

*The 2S3 self-propelled gun (Tim Ripley)*

THE **2S3** SELF-PROPELLED GUN (also known as the **Akatsiya** (Acacia) and in the West as the **M1973**) entered into service with the USSR armed forces in the early 1970s. The 2S3 is based on the chassis of the SA-4 Ganef SAM system, although with six rather than seven road wheels on each side. The six-man crew includes the driver housed beside the engine compartment at the front of the vehicle, two ammunition handlers at the rear of the hull and the turret crew. The ammunition is passed to the turret crew through two circular hatches in the rear of the hull. The large power-operated turret, on which the 152.4 mm gun/howitzer is mounted, is also at the rear and houses the commander's cupola on its left-hand side. Manufactured by the Russian state arsenals, the 2S3 has been sold to a number of countries and is in service with armed forces in Algeria, Cuba, Iraq, Libya and Vietnam, as well as with the Russian Army and a number of former republics of the USSR. There are no known variants, and manufacture has ceased.

The **2S1**, or **Gvozdika** (Carnation), self-propelled gun was also introduced into the USSR's armed forces in the early 1970s. Known in the West as the **M1974**, its first public showing was in 1974, and although production is now complete, the 2S1, which was manufactured in state factories in the USSR, Bulgaria and Poland, has been sold to armed forces in Algeria, Angola, Bulgaria, Croatia, Cuba, the Czech Republic, Ethiopia, Finland, Hungary, Iran, Iraq, Libya, Poland, Romania, Slovakia, Syria, Yemen and Yugoslavia, as well as being in service with the Russian Army and a number of former republics of the USSR. The construction of the 2S1 uses many components in common with the MT-LB multi-purpose tracked vehicle developed in the USSR in the late 1960s, and has a similar low-profile turret mounted at the rear of a long hull. The 122 mm howitzer is mounted in the power-operated turret. There is a crew of four, with the driver's compartment and engine compartment located forward in the hull. The adjustable suspension has seven large road wheels, and the vehicle is fully amphibious, being propelled in the water by its tracks. There are a number of variants of the 2S1, including artillery command and reconnaissance vehicles (known as the MT-LBus/1V12 series), as well as radar, mine-clearing and chemical reconnaissance vehicles.

*Polish 2S1 Gvozdika self-propelled howitzers on exercise on Drawsko Pomorski training area (VS-Books Carl Schulze)*

## SPECIFICATION:

**2S3**

**Crew:** 6

**Armament:** 1 x 152.4 mm main gun, 1 x 7.62 mm AA machine-gun

**Ammunition:** 46 rounds, 152.4 mm; 1,500 rounds, 7.62 mm

**Dimensions:** length (gun forwards) 8.40 m, (hull) 7.77 m; height 3.05 m; width 3.25 m; ground clearance 0.45 m

**Weight:** loaded 27,500 kg; ground pressure 0.59 kg/cm²

**Engine:** V-59 V-12 water-cooled diesel; output 520 hp

**Performance:** range 500 km; maximum speed 60 km/h; speed cross-country 40 km/h

**Armour:** steel – 15 mm max. turret, 20 mm max. hull

## SPECIFICATION:

**2S1**

**Crew:** 4

**Armament:** 1 x 122 mm main gun

**Ammunition:** 40 rounds, 122 mm

**Dimensions:** length 7.62 m; height 2.73 m; width 2.85 m; ground clearance 0.40 m

**Weight:** loaded 15,700 kg; ground pressure 0.49 kg/cm²

**Engine:** YaMZ-238, V-8 water-cooled diesel; output 300 hp

**Performance:** range 500 km; maximum speed 61.5 km/h; speed cross-country 40 km/h

**Armour:** steel – est. 20 mm max.

# AAAV and AAV7 APC/AIFV

*The AAAV (Advanced Amphibious Assault Vehicle)*

THE **LVTP7** (LANDING VEHICLE, Tracked Personnel, Model 7) **AAAV** (Advanced Amphibious Assault Vehicle) was developed in the mid-1960s by the then FMC Corporation as a replacement for the US armed forces' **LVTP5** series. Following trials of the prototype (**LVTPX12**), the first production models were delivered in 1971 by the United Defense LP (previously the FMC Corporation) based in San José, California, USA. Production ceased in 1974, but the vehicle is still in service with the US armed forces, including the Marine Corps which has designated the vehicle as **AAV7**, although General Dynamics is developing a replacement Advanced Amphibious Assault Vehicle for the Marines. The AAAV has also been sold abroad to Argentina, Brazil, Italy, South Korea, Spain, Thailand and Venezuela.

The boat-shaped welded aluminium hull carries a crew of three, as well as having space for 25 troops. The engine compartment is to the front, on the right-hand side, with the 12.7 mm machine-gun turret behind. The driver sits at the front left with the periscope extending through his cupola roof, and the commander sits to the rear, with his cupola positioned behind the driver's hatch. Entry to the troop compartment, which extends to the back of the hull, is via a power-operated ramp at the rear, but overhead hatches can also be used for loading troops or supplies. The AAAV is fully amphibious, using its tracks or two water jets on either side of the hull to propel it through the water.

From 1986/7 an upgraded version for the US forces, which is called the **AAV7A1**, has had a replacement turret fitted called the Upgunned Weapons Station, armed with a 40 mm grenade launcher, as well as a 12.7 mm machine-gun. Other improvements include a replacement Cummins engine, smoke generators, passive night vision equipment and an improved electric weapon station. As well as this Service Life Extension Program (SLEP), a number of new vehicles were built up to 1986 to these AAV7A1 specifications, some of these that were ordered by the Marine Corps being fitted with the Enhanced Appliqué Armor Kit (EAAK). Specialised variants include the **AAVC7A1** command model, with extensive communications equipment but without the machine-gun cupola, the **AAVR7A1** recovery model, also without the machine-gun cupola but with a range of equipment including a winch and a crane, and the **AAV7A1** mine-clearer, which fires rockets into the minefield from a kit bolted to the roof of the troop compartment.

## SPECIFICATION:

**AAV7**

**Crew:** 3 + 25

**Armament:** 1 x 12.7 mm machine-gun

**Ammunition:** 1,000 rounds, 12.7 mm

**Dimensions:** length 7.94 m; height (overall) 3.26 m, (hull roof) 3.12 m; width 3.27 m; ground clearance 0.41 m

**Weight:** empty 17,441 kg; loaded 22,838 kg

**Engine:** Detroit Diesel model 8V-53T, 8-cylinder, water-cooled turbo-charged diesel; output 400 hp

**Performance:** range 482 km; maximum speed 64 km/h

**Armour:** aluminium – 45 mm max.

*The AAV7A1 is in service with the US Marine Corps*

# ISRAEL
# Achzarit APC/AIFV

F OLLOWING THE DEVELOPMENT OF the Israeli-developed and built Merkava Main Battle Tank (MBT), the Israeli Defence Forces decided that it needed to develop its own well-protected infantry armoured vehicle which could operate with the Merkava. Development was based on the heavily modified chassis of the Russian T-54/T-55 MBT with the turret removed, and the first prototype was completed in 1987. Following trials the **Achzarit** was ordered by the Israeli Defence Forces, and production at the Israel Ordnance Corps factory at Tel a Shomer started in 1988.

The significant feature of the Achzarit is its extra layer of Israeli-developed passive armour mounted on the chassis, which makes it the best-protected Armoured Personnel Carrier/Armoured Infantry Fighting Vehicle (APC/AIFV) in the world. The Achzarit carries a crew of three plus up to seven infantry in its rebuilt chassis. The crew consists of the driver seated in his compartment at the front left of the hull, the commander to his right and the gunner seated at the front right. The gunner operates the RAFAEL Overhead Weapon Station – a 7.62 mm M240 machine-gun which can be aimed and fired by remote control from within the vehicle. A further three 7.62 mm pintle-mounted machine-guns are provided, one being mounted on the commander's hatch at the front of the hull, and two over the troop compartment at the centre of the hull top. The troop compartment is situated in the middle of the vehicle and holds seven infantry who are seated three-a-side with one in the centre. Access to the troop compartment is via a hydraulically operated clamshell door in the hull rear on the right. The top half of the door opens upwards, while the bottom half folds down to reach the ground. The three crew members each have their own hatch in the hull front, and the troop compartment can also be accessed by two hatches in the hull roof. The engine compartment is situated at the rear left of the hull, the specially designed compact power-pack

*An Achzarit AIFV of the Israeli Defence Forces*

allowing room for a passageway between the troop compartment and the exit at the rear. The **Achzarit Mk 1** is fitted with a transversely mounted Detroit Diesel 8V-71 TTA water-cooled two-stroke V-8 diesel engine, but the latest production version, the **Achzarit 2**, has been upgraded to a Detroit Diesel 8V-92 TA diesel engine, giving an improved power-to-weight ratio and greater acceleration. The original T-54/T-55 suspension has also been upgraded to give the Achzarit greater cross-country mobility, comparable with the latest Israeli MBTs.

Standard equipment for the Achzarit includes night vision equipment, a fire detection and suppression system and an NBC (Nuclear, Biological, Chemical) system. The only known Achzarit variant is a command post vehicle with additional specialised communications equipment but with the roof-mounted machine-guns removed. The Achzarit is in service only with the Israeli Defence Forces.

## SPECIFICATION:
**Achzarit APC/AIFV**
**Crew:** 3 + 7
**Armament:** 4 x 7.62 mm machine-guns, 6 x smoke grenade launchers
**Dimensions:** height (to hull top) approx 2.00 m; width 3.64 m
**Weight:** loaded 44,000 kg
**Engine:** (Mk 1) Detroit Diesel 8V-71 TTA diesel; output 650 hp
**Engine:** (Mk 2) Detroit Diesel 8V-92 TA diesel; output 850 hp
**Armour:** passive composite

# ADATS SP Artillery

*An ADATS missile system stands guard against air attack in the Middle East*

THE **M113** SERIES OF ARMOURED PERSONNEL carriers is manufactured by the US United Defense Ground Systems Divisions, San José, California, and has been in production since 1960. It is one of the most widely used armoured fighting vehicles in the world, being relatively cheap to produce and extremely adaptable to a wide range of modifications and weapon systems. In 1964 the **M113A1** superseded the M113 in production, with the M113's Chrysler petrol engine being replaced by the more fuel-efficient General Motors Detroit Diesel Model 6V-53 diesel engine with Allison semi-automatic transmission, the diesel engine giving greater mobility and also reducing the risk of fire. The vehicle has been further upgraded as the **M113A2**, including improved suspension, and the **M113A3**, which first entered service in 1987, with a more powerful engine, spall liners and appliqué armour.

The hull of the M113 is all-welded aluminium armour. The two crew members are positioned at the front of the vehicle: the driver is seated front left with the engine compartment to his right, and the commander behind with a hatch on the roof. The troop compartment is at the rear of the vehicle and carries up to eleven infantry, seated along each side of the compartment. Access to the troop compartment is via a large power-operated ramp at the hull rear or a roof hatch. The standard M113 has an M2 12.7 mm machine-gun mounted on a cupola on the roof, although there are many variations of armament fitted to the numerous M113s in service, including 7.62 mm machine-guns, 20 mm/76 mm cannon, 81 mm/120 mm mortars, smoke dischargers and anti-tank and anti-aircraft missiles. The basic M113 is also fully amphibious, being propelled through the water by its

tracks. Before entering the water the bilge pumps are switched on and a hinged trim vane raised at the front of the hull. Optional extra equipment includes an NBC system, night vision equipment and additional armour protection.

The Canadian ADATS (Air Defense Anti-Tank System) self-propelled artillery is mounted on a modified M113A2 APC chassis. The system comprises two banks of four Oerlikon Aerospace surface-to-air missiles carried either side of an unmanned power-operated turret mounted on the top of the hull roof. The self-propelled M113A2 with ADATS is in service only with the Canadian armed forces. The Canadian Army also has a wide range of more standard M113s, M113A1s and M113A2s, with M113A3s and an upgraded MTVL (mobile tactical vehicle light) on order.

## SPECIFICATION:

**Crew:** 2 + 11
**Armament:** (standard M113A2) 1 x 12.7 mm machine-gun, (Canadian ADATS) 8 x ADATS surface-to-air missiles
**Ammunition:** 2,000 rounds, 12.7 mm
**Dimensions:** length 4.86 m; height (overall) 2.52 m, (hull top) 1.85 m; width 2.69 m; ground clearance 0.43 m
**Weight:** empty 9,957 kg; loaded 11,253 kg; ground pressure 0.55 kg/cm²
**Engine:** Detroit Diesel Model 6V-53 6-cylinder water-cooled diesel; output 212 hp
**Performance:** range 483 km; maximum speed 68 km/h; speed cross-country 50 km/h
**Armour:** aluminium – 12 mm–38 mm

# Alvis 8 Mamba APC/AIFV

T HE **ALVIS 8 MAMBA** HAS BEEN DEVELOPED
from the South African National Defence Force's
**Mamba Mk II** (following on from the successful
**Mamba Mk I**) 4 x 4 APC. The original **Mamba 4 x 2**
armour-protected vehicle was developed and built by
Mechem Consultants, South Africa, and further
development by the Reumech OMC company in
South Africa led to the 4 x 4 Mamba II mine-protected
vehicle being produced for the South African Defence
Force, wherever possible using standard vehicle
components from the well proved Mercedes-Benz
range of UNIMOG cross-country civil and military
vehicles. In 1999 Reumech OMC was taken over by
Vickers Defence Systems of the UK (now Vickers
OMC), and production of the South African Mamba II
has ceased. The first British Alvis 8 Mambas were
produced by the Coventry-based company Alvis
Vehicles, in conjunction with Reumech OMC, the first
interim vehicles being supplied in 1996 by Reumech
OMC, with subsequent vehicles being produced
under licence by Alvis. In 1999 production at the Alvis
site was transferred to the former GKN Defence
facility at Telford, UK.

The Alvis 8 Mamba has been developed to provide
a high level of protection against anti-tank mines with
an all-welded steel monocoque hull. The armoured
hull also provides protection against small-arms and
shell splinters, and further protection is provided by
the bullet-proof windows at the front, sides and rear.
Additional wire-mesh protection can also be fitted to
the windows. The vehicle has a crew of two, with the
driver (right) and commander (left) seated behind the
engine compartment at the front. The troop
compartment extends to the rear of the hull and
carries nine infantry seated either side of the
compartment. Integral firing ports can be fitted in the
windows in the troop compartment. Normal access
for the crew and troops is via a large door at the rear
of the hull, although there are six roof hatches in the

*Mamba APC in service with the British Army in Bosnia*

troop compartment and one roof hatch above the
driver and commander's position. Optional extra
equipment includes a roof-mounted 12.7 mm
machine-gun, smoke grenade launchers, night vision
equipment, run-flat tyres, roof-mounted equipment,
including a winch, and a variety of radio communications and suppression equipment. There is also a
light short-wheelbase version, the **Alvis 4**, which has
been produced for the British Army for liaison,
reconnaissance and command/control duties.

The Alvis 8 Mamba is in service only with the
British Army, with a number being used by Royal
Engineers Explosive Ordnance Disposal (EOD) teams
mine-clearing in the former Yugoslavia.

*Mamba APCs undergoing user trials*

### SPECIFICATION:

**Crew:** 2 + 9
**Armament:** 1 x 12.7 mm machine-gun (optional)
**Dimensions:** length 5.53 m; height 2.60 m; width 2.21 m;
ground clearance 0.38m
**Weight:** empty 5,710 kg; loaded 7,500 kg
**Engine:** Mercedes-Benz OM 352 6-cylinder water-cooled
diesel; output 123 hp
**Performance:** range 900 km; maximum speed 110 km/h;
speed cross-country 80 km/h
**Armour:** steel

# Alvis Stormer APC/IFV Family and Starstreak SP AA Artillery

*An Alvis Starstreak air defence system at speed*

THE PROTOTYPE OF THE **ALVIS STORMER** armoured personnel carrier, known as **FV4333**, was built in the 1970s by a UK government research and development organisation. The prototype used many basic components from the Alvis Scorpion range of CVR(T) (Combat Vehicle Reconnaissance [Tracked]), particularly the Spartan, but further development by the Alvis company led to the Stormer range. The vehicle entered production in 1981 and is still being manufactured by Alvis Vehicles Ltd in Telford, UK.

The Stormer carries a three-man crew, as well as being able to accommodate up to eight (reduced from the ten that the prototype FV4333 could carry) troops in the rear compartment, with their equipment stored in stowage boxes attached to the side of the hull, enabling them to operate from the vehicle for 24 hours on the battlefield. A large door on the right of the vertical hull rear allows access to the troop compartment. The driver's position is at the front left of the vehicle, with the engine compartment to the right. In most variants the weapon station is on the front part of the roof top, where the turrets can carry a range of machine-guns (7.62 mm and 12.7 mm), cannon (20 mm, 25 mm and 30 mm) or guns (up to 76 mm or 90 mm). The hatches are normally situated immediately behind the weapon station.

The highly mobile Alvis Stormer has been used in a wide variety of roles by the British Army, including air defence with guns and missiles, ambulance, minelayer, mortar carrier (81 mm or 120 mm), command/control, engineer vehicle or recovery vehicle. The vehicle range is fitted with a choice of turrets, including the Helio FVT900 with 20 mm Oerlikon Contraves cannon and a 7.62 mm machine-gun, and the Thyssen Henschel TH-1 with twin 7.62 mm machine-guns. In 1986 a number of Stormers in the British Army were fitted with the Shorts **Starstreak** High Velocity Missile (HVM) system: they have an unmanned turret and eight ready-to-launch Starstreak surface-to-air missiles. Optional extra equipment includes an NBC system, a night vision system, a flotation screen and firing ports.

As well as being in service with the British Army, the Stormer has been sold to Indonesia, Malaysia and Oman. Alvis also built a flatbed variant for Operation 'Desert Storm' in the Gulf War to carry the GIAT Minotaur mine-scattering system. A further new variant, called the **Shielder**, is being built with Alliant Technosystems Volcano.

*Alvis Starstreak with its HVMs ready to fire*

*Alvis Starstreak HVM of the British 12th Regiment Royal Artillery (VS-Books Carl Schulze)*

## SPECIFICATION:

**Stormer APC**
**Crew:** 3 + 8
**Armament:** a wide range, including 7.62 mm or 12.7 mm machine-gun, 20 mm, 25 mm or 30 mm cannon
**Ammunition:** varies with armament
**Dimensions:** length 5.27 m; height 2.27 m; width 2.76 m, (including stowage boxes); ground clearance 0.43 m
**Weight:** loaded 12,700 kg; ground pressure 0.40 kg/cm$^2$
**Engine:** Perkins T6/3544 water-cooled 6-cylinder turbo-charged diesel; output 250 hp
**Performance:** range 650 km; maximum speed 80 km/h; speed cross-country 50 km/h
**Armour:** aluminium

# AMX-10 APC/AIFV

*AMX-10P of the French Army armed with a 20 mm cannon and 7.62 mm machine-gun*

THE **AMX-10** RANGE OF MECHANISED infantry combat vehicles built for the French Army shows the development of the armoured personnel carrier into an armoured infantry fighting vehicle which can be adapted to multiple purposes, carrying a 20 mm cannon and able to operate as an anti-tank guided missile launcher. The **AMX-10P** was developed in the mid-1960s by Atelier de Construction d'Issy-les-Moulineaux (AMX) for the French Army, with the first prototype completed in 1968. The first production vehicles were delivered in 1973, being built by GIAT Industries in Roanne.

The three-man crew comprises the driver, positioned upper front left with the engine compartment to the right, and the gunner and commander in the two-man power-operated turret, which has night vision equipment. A further eight troops can be carried in the infantry compartment to the rear which is accessed by a large power-operated ramp; the troops also have roof hatches and periscopes. There are two firing ports in the rear ramp but none in the sides of the troop compartment. The turret is in the centre of the roof and carries a 20 mm cannon, a 7.62 mm coaxial machine-gun and smoke grenade dischargers; two outward-opening hatches are positioned behind the turret. The vehicle is fitted with an NBC system. The **AMX-10P** also has a water propulsion system, driving the vehicle with water jets positioned either side of the hull at the rear, making it fully amphibious. A Marine version has been built specifically for amphibious operations which is fitted with a 12.7 mm machine-gun turret, a 25 mm Dragar turret or a 90 mm TS-90 turret.

There are a large number of AMX-10 variants, including the anti-tank **AMX-10P HOT** version which

has four HOT Anti-Tank Guided Weapons (ATGWs) fitted on the turret, a version with RATAC (radar for field artillery fire) fitted on the roof, an artillery observation vehicle, a survey vehicle and an observer vehicle (respectively the **AMX-10P SAO**, **AMX-10 SAT** and **AMX-10 VOA**), the **AMX-10 TM** mortar tractor, a command vehicle (**AMX-10 PC**), a driver training vehicle, a repair vehicle (**AMX-10 ECH**) and an ambulance. The AMX-10P series is still in production and has now replaced the AMX VCI Infantry Combat Vehicle (developed in the 1950s) in front line service in the French Army. It has also been sold to Indonesia (Marine version), Iraq, Qatar, Saudi Arabia, Singapore (Marine version) and the United Arab Emirates.

## SPECIFICATION:

**AMX-10P APC**

**Crew:** 3 + 8

**Armament:** 1 x 20 mm cannon, 1 x coaxial 7.62 mm machine-gun, 4 x smoke dischargers

**Ammunition:** 760 rounds, 20 mm; 2,000 rounds 7.62 mm

**Dimensions:** length 5.90 m; height (overall) 2.83 m, (hull top) 1.95 m; width 2.83 m; ground clearance 0.45 m

**Weight:** empty 12,700 kg; loaded 14,500 kg; ground pressure 0.53 kg/cm²

**Engine:** Hispano-Suiza HS-115 V-8 water-cooled supercharged diesel; output 260 hp

**Performance:** range 500 km; maximum speed 65 km/h; speed cross-country 45 km/h

**Armour:** aluminium

# AMX-10RC Light Tank/Recce Vehicle

*AMX-10RC of the French Army in the reconnaissance role*

BY THE LATE 1960S THE FRENCH ARMY needed a replacement long-range armoured vehicle to take over from the 8 x 8 Panhard EBR 75. Developed in the 1970s by GIAT, this wheeled reconnaissance variant of the AMX-10P – the **AMX-10RC** – is designed to move rapidly cross-country with its 6 x 6 drive layout. The first prototype was completed in 1971, and production was started in 1978 by Atelier de Construction Roanne. The vehicle is well armed with a 105 mm main gun, firing HEAT (High Explosive Anti-Tank), HE (High Explosive) or APFSDs (Armour Piercing Fin-Stabilised, Discarding Sabot) rounds, making it a match for most of today's medium tanks, which is necessary as it is intended to be able to counter enemy armour well ahead of the main force. Although lightly armoured, its high power-to-weight ratio gives it good speed and mobility and, in order to maximise the space within the hull, it deploys a skid-steer system in which the vehicle is manoeuvred in the same way as a tracked vehicle, by speeding up one side and slowing down the other, with all the wheels being powered. The hydro-pneumatic suspension is also a unique feature, allowing the driver to adjust the suspension for the entire vehicle, or just one side, or just the front or rear, according to the ground clearance required for that particular terrain. As with the AMX-10P, the French Army version has a water propulsion system comprising two water jets mounted on either side of the hull rear, which makes it fully amphibious and gives it a maximum speed in the water of 7.2 km/h. The computerised fire control system includes a laser rangefinder and LLLTV (Low Light Level Television) system with displays for the gunner and commander. It is also fitted with night vision equipment and an NBC system.

The AMX-10RC is in service with the French Army, final deliveries being made in 1987, and has also been sold to the armed forces in Morocco and Qatar. It saw action in the Gulf War in 1991, and has also been deployed on occasions by the French *Force d'Action Rapide* (FAR), for example in Chad. There is a driver trainer vehicle variant, and the French Army is planning to upgrade the AMX-10RC. Among the range of possible improvements are the installation of a 105 mm gun able to fire NATO types of ammunition, additional armour, a decoy system, a thermal camera, a land battlefield management system and an electronic control system for the transmission.

## SPECIFICATION:

**AMX-10RC**
**Crew:** 4
**Armament:** 1 x 105 mm main gun, 1 x 7.62 mm coaxial machine-gun, 4 x smoke dischargers
**Ammunition:** 38 rounds, 105 mm; 4,000 rounds, 7.62 mm
**Dimensions:** length (including main armament) 9.15 m, (hull) 6.38 m; height (overall) 2.68 m, (turret top) 2.29 m; width 2.95 m; ground clearance 0.35 m (normal)
**Weight:** empty 14,900 kg; combat 15,880 kg
**Engine:** Hispano-Suiza HS-115 supercharged water-cooled 8-cylinder diesel; output 260 hp, also Baudouin Model 6F 11 SRX diesel, 280 hp
**Performance:** range 1,000 km; maximum speed 85 km/h; speed cross-country 50 km/h
**Armour:** aluminium

# AMX-13 Light Tank/Recce Vehicle

*AMX-13 light tank armed with a 105 mm gun*

DEVELOPED SOON AFTER THE END OF World War II, the French **AMX-13** is one of the most successful postwar tank designs in the world. The light tank was designed at the Atelier de Construction d'Issy-les-Moulineaux (AMX) and built first by the Atelier de Construction Roanne from 1952 before being taken over by Creusot-Loire at Chalon-sur-Saône in the 1960s. Later models were constructed at Atelier de Construction Roanne after GIAT Industries took over Creusot-Loire. Although the tank was originally intended to provide airborne forces with medium-fire support transportable by aircraft, it was never used in that role and instead became the standard light tank of the ground-based French Army for many years, being used as a tank destroyer and reconnaissance vehicle. An innovatory feature, which first appeared on the 1948 prototype of the AMX-13, is its Fives-Cail Babcock FL-10 oscillating turret. The turret is designed in two parts: the fixed bottom part is mounted on the turret ring and has two trunnions which carry the oscillating upper part on which the gun is rigidly mounted. The design allows an automatic loader to be fitted, thus keeping the number of crew down to three, rather than the standard four, without any loss of fighting capability. The turret design and three-man crew also enable the tank to have a low-profile, although this does impose a maximum height on crew members of 1.73 m (5 ft 8 in).

Because of its length in service, the basic AMX-13 design has been revised over the years. Early models were fitted with a 75 mm gun firing HE or HEAT rounds; later models have either a 90 mm or 105 mm gun. The engine on many AMX-13s has also latterly been converted from its original petrol to diesel. The tank's versatility has also been shown by the range of variants that have been produced from the basic AMX-13 chassis, including being adapted as an APC,

a bridge-layer, a rocket launcher, an Armoured Recovery Vehicle (ARV) and an engineer vehicle. GIAT and a number of other companies abroad offer upgrades of the AMX-13, including the option of passive night vision equipment, extra armour, improved fire control systems and a laser rangefinder.

Although production finished in the 1980s and the vehicle is now withdrawn from service by the French Army, the AMX-13 is still in use today with many armed forces around the world, chiefly Singapore, where Singapore Technologies Automotive has rebuilt most of its vehicles with a new engine, cooling system and transmission, but also Argentina, the Dominican Republic, Ecuador, Indonesia, Ivory Coast, Lebanon, Peru and Venezuela.

## SPECIFICATION:

**Crew:** 3

**Armament:** 1 x 75 mm (later 90 mm or 105 mm) main gun, 1 x 7.5 mm or 7.62 mm coaxial machine-gun, 4 x smoke grenade dischargers

**Ammunition:** 37 rounds, 75 mm; 32 rounds, 90 mm; 3,600 rounds, 7.62 mm

**Dimensions:** length (gun forward) 6.36 m, (hull) 4.88 m; height (to commander's hatch) 2.30 m; width 2.51 m; ground clearance 0.37 m

**Weight:** empty 13,000 kg; loaded 15,000 kg; ground pressure 0.76 kg/cm$^2$

**Engine:** SOFAM Model 8Gxb 8-cylinder water-cooled petrol; output 250 hp

**Performance:** range 400 km; maximum speed 60 km/h; speed cross-country 45 km/h

**Armour:** welded steel – 10–40 mm

# AMX-30 and AMX-30 155 mm GCT SP Howitzer SP Artillery

THE **AMX-30 GCT** SELF-PROPELLED GUN was developed for the French Army using the chassis of the AMX-30 main battle tank which was produced from the mid-1960s by the government-owned Atelier de Construction Roanne. In 1969, the prototype 155 mm GCT (*Grande Cadence de Tir*) was developed to replace the 105 mm Mk 61 and the 155 mm Mk 3 self-propelled guns then in service with the French Army, and production started in 1977 at GIAT Industries, Roanne, with the first vehicles delivered the following year.

The 155 mm gun with double-baffle muzzle brake is mounted on a large, fully enclosed, flat-sided turret on the centre of the chassis. Also mounted are a 7.62 mm or 12.7 mm anti-aircraft machine-gun and two smoke grenade dischargers. The chassis has five road wheels on either side, an idler at the front and drive sprocket at the rear, and four track-return rollers. The upper part of the suspension can be covered with a skirt. The main gun overhangs the front of the chassis and has powered elevation, and the powered turret traverses through 360 degrees. The gun is fed by a fully automatic loader at a rate of eight rounds per minute but can also be loaded manually at three rounds per minute. The standard 155 mm ME M107 projectile has a range of 18,000 m, but the option of other projectiles includes anti-tank mines, and extended-range smoke and illuminating projectiles. The vehicle has a crew of four and is fitted with an NBC system. The driver has night vision equipment.

The 155 mm GCT is still in production (although the production of the **AMX-30 MBT** has ceased, as the tank is being superseded by the GIAT Leclerc MBT) and is in service with the French Army. It has also been sold to Saudi Arabia, Kuwait and, before the Gulf War, Iraq. There are no variants, although the self-propelled gun can be fitted with a range of fire-control systems and the French have trialled the GCT turret fitted on to a Russian T-72 MBT chassis. The current Hispano-Suiza engine is also due to be replaced by a Renault E9 diesel engine.

*AMX-30 EM MBT of the Spanish Army*

*Self-propelled howitzer 155 mm GCT in Bosnia (VS-Books Carl Schulze)*

## SPECIFICATION:

**155 mm GCT**
**Crew:** 4
**Armament:** 1 x 155 mm gun, 1 x 7.62 mm or 12.7 mm AA machine-gun, 4 x smoke grenade dischargers
**Ammunition:** 42 rounds, 155 mm; 2,050 rounds, 7.62 mm or 800 rounds, 12.7 mm
**Dimensions:** length (gun forwards) 10.25 m, (hull) 6.70 m; height 3.25 m; width 3.15 m; ground clearance 0.42 m
**Weight:** empty 38,000 kg; loaded 42,000 kg
**Engine:** Hispano-Suiza HS 110 12-cylinder water-cooled supercharged multi-fuel; output 720 hp
**Performance:** range 450 km; maximum speed 60 km/h; speed cross-country 40 km/h
**Armour:** steel – 20 mm max.

# Ariete C1 MBT

*Ariete C1 MBT of the Italian Army at speed*

THE **ARIETE C1**, WHICH ENTERED SERVICE in 1995, is an Italian-designed and built main battle tank. After World War II the Italian Army had first used the US M47 then the M60A1 and the German Leopard 1. Although the Italians had by this time built their own MBT (the OF-40), this was designed only for export to the United Arab Emirates. In 1982 the Italian Army decided it needed a new MBT, which it stipulated should be manufactured in Italy. The company Otobreda, in consortium with Iveco Fiat, was awarded the contract and the first prototype was delivered in 1986. A further five prototypes were completed by 1986, and the Italian Army has subsequently ordered 200 vehicles, to be manufactured at the Otobreda factory at La Spezia, Italy, with the power-pack and the automotive components being supplied by Iveco Fiat. Delivery of the Ariete C1 is due to be completed in 2002, and a

Mk 2 version of the Ariete MBT is currently under development. There are no variants.

Otobreda has also designed and manufactured the 120 mm smooth-bore main gun, which fires APFSDS and HEAT-MP (High Explosive Anti-Tank – Multi-Purpose) rounds and is fully stabilised. The tube is fitted with a muzzle reference system and fume extractor, and is covered with a thermal sleeve. Also mounted on the turret is a 7.62 mm coaxial machine-gun, a 7.62 mm anti-aircraft machine-gun and eight smoke grenade dischargers. The tank carries the conventional number of four crew in its all-welded steel hull. The driver is situated forward under the glacis plate, to the right; the remainder of the crew are in the power-operated turret, with the gunner and commander to the right of the main gun and the loader to the left. The engine is situated at the rear. The tank has a distinctive low profile with its

*The Italian Army has 200 Ariete C1 MBTs*

flat-roofed turret sharply angled to the front and rear. The commander's cupola is on the right side of the roof with a large periscope sight to its front. The gunner's sight is located right forward on the turret. The suspension comprises seven road wheels each side, and the upper part is covered by a skirt. The Galileo computerised fire-control system includes day/night sights and a laser rangefinder. The tank is also fitted with an NBC system.

## SPECIFICATION:

**Crew:** 4

**Armament:** 1 x 120 mm gun, 1 x 7.62 mm coaxial machine-gun, 1 x 7.62 mm anti-aircraft machine-gun, 8 x smoke dischargers

**Ammunition:** 42 rounds, 120 mm, including smoke and illuminating rounds; 2,400 rounds, 7.72 mm

**Dimensions:** length (gun forward) 9.52 m, (hull) 7.59 m; height (to turret roof) 2.45 m; width 3.6 m; ground clearance 0.44 m

**Weight:** loaded 54,000 kg; ground pressure 0.85 kg/cm$^2$

**Engine:** Iveco V-12 MTCA turbo-charged intercooled 12-cylinder diesel; output 1,300 hp

**Performance:** range 550 km; maximum speed 65 km/h; speed cross-country 50 km/h

**Armour:** steel, with composite 'advanced armour' on nose and glacis plate

# AS-90 SP Artillery

*AS-90s of the British Army fire their 155 mm guns during a firepower demonstration in Bosnia*

THE FIRST PROTOTYPE OF THE **AS-90** self-propelled gun was built in 1981 by Vickers Shipbuilding and Engineering (VSEL) at its facility in Barrow-in-Furness, UK. The 155 mm artillery turret was called the GBT 155 and the company subsequently privately developed a new complete 155 mm artillery system called the AS-90, the first of two prototypes being completed in 1986. In 1989 the British Army chose the AS-90 to replace all its other self-propelled guns and placed its first orders. The final deliveries of a total order of 179 were made in 1986 by Marconi Marine, Land and Naval Systems, which had taken over Vickers, with the vehicles still being manufactured in Barrow-in-Furness.

The AS-90 has a crew of five. The driver is positioned at the front left, with the raised engine compartment front right. The turret is at the back of the chassis and is accessed by a large door in the chassis rear. The AS-90 has hydropneumatic suspension with six dual rubber-tyred road wheels either side, a drive sprocket at the front, an idler at the rear and three track-return rollers. The large 155 mm/39 calibre ordnance has a double-baffle muzzle brake and is held when travelling by a lock pivoted on the front of the chassis. The ordnance has a maximum range of 24,700 m using standard ammunition, which

can be extended to over 30,000 m using extended-range full-bore ammunition. Two rounds per minute is the rate of fire for sustained firing but three rounds in ten seconds can be achieved in bursts. Of the 48 155 mm projectiles carried, 31 are stored in the turret bustle magazine. Additional armament comprises a 7.62 mm anti-aircraft machine-gun and ten smoke grenade dischargers. The vehicle is also fitted with an NBC system and passive night vision equipment, as well as standard British Army systems such as muzzle-velocity measuring equipment, a land navigation system and a fully automatic gun-laying capability. There are no variants of the 155 mm AS-90, although Marconi has proposed the chassis for a number of other uses, including maintenance, recovery and flatbed vehicles. It is also planned to fit some of the British Army's AS-90s with a 155 mm/52 calibre barrel. The Indian Army has also trialled the AS-90 turret fitted onto the T-72 MBT chassis.

*An AS-90 of the British Army at speed*

*An AS-90 of the Royal Artillery takes up a firing position in Bosnia*

## SPECIFICATION:

**Crew:** 5
**Armament:** 1 x 155 mm gun, 1 x 7.62 mm AA machine-gun, 10 x smoke grenade dischargers
**Ammunition:** 48 rounds, 155 mm; 1,000 rounds, 7.62 mm
**Dimensions:** length (gun forwards) 9.90 m, (hull) 7.20 m; height 3.00 m; width 3.40 m; ground clearance 0.41 m
**Weight:** loaded 45,000 kg; ground pressure 0.90 kg/cm$^2$
**Engine:** Cummins VTA 903T 660T-660 V-8 diesel; output 660 hp
**Performance:** range 370 km; maximum speed 55 km/h; speed cross-country 45 km/h
**Armour:** steel – 17 mm max.

# ASCOD APC/AIFV

*ASCOD AIFV armed with a 30 mm cannon and smoke dischargers on each side of the turret*

THE **ASCOD** (AUSTRIAN–SPANISH Co-Operative Development) APC/AIFV was developed jointly by Steyr-Daimler-Puch of Austria and Santa Barbara of Spain. The first prototype was completed in 1990, and following trials of a number of other prototypes, in 1996 Spain placed the first production order for 144 ASCODs, and the vehicle is now in service with the Spanish Army under the name **Pizarro**. The Austrian Army has also ordered 112 of the vehicles, under the name **Ulan**.

The ASCOD has a crew of three, with the driver seated at the front left and the engine compartment positioned front right. The two-man power-operated turret is behind the driver in the centre of the hull, on the right-hand side. The vehicle has all-welded steel armour but its thickness is unknown. Spanish ASCODs are also likely to be fitted with ERA (Explosive Reactive Armour) developed by Santa Barbara. The turret is armed with a stabilised 30 mm cannon with a coaxial 7.62 mm machine-gun mounted to the left of the cannon, and 12 smoke grenade launchers. The turret traverse is a full 360 degrees and has a weapon elevation from –10 degrees to +50 degrees. The troop compartment is to the rear of the hull and can accommodate eight infantry. Access to the troop compartment is via a large door in the vertical hull rear, opening to the right, and there is a large stowage bin on either side of the door. The suspension on each side has seven road wheels, a drive sprocket at the front, an idler at the back and track return rollers. The upper part of the suspension is covered by a wavy skirt.

The ASCOD's standard equipment includes an NBC system, night vision equipment, appliqué armour and a computerised day/night fire-control system. A dozer blade or a mine-clearing plough can also be mounted on the front of the vehicle. There are a number of variants of the ASCOD, including an anti-tank version with various ATGW systems, an armoured mortar carrier, an armoured engineer vehicle, an armoured command vehicle, an armoured recovery and repair vehicle, an armoured logistics carrier, an ambulance, a light tank with a 105 mm gun and a further 105 mm variant fitted with the General Dynamics Low-Profile Turret (LPT) has been trialled. Various alternative weapon systems can be fitted, including an additional 120 mm mortar system, SAM (surface-to-air missile) and SPAAG (self-propelled anti-aircraft gun).

## SPECIFICATION:

**Crew:** 3 + 8
**Armament:** 1 x 25 mm or 30 mm gun, 1 x 7.62 mm coaxial machine-gun, 12 x smoke grenade launchers
**Ammunition:** 402 rounds, 30 mm; 2,900 rounds, 7.62 mm
**Dimensions:** length 6.99 m; height (hull top) 2.65 m, (turret top) 2.65 m; width 3.15 m; ground clearance 0.45 m
**Weight:** loaded 27,500 kg
**Engine:** MTU 8V 183 TE22 V-90 V-8 diesel; output 600 hp
**Performance:** range 600 km; maximum speed 70 km/h; speed cross-country 50 km/h
**Armour:** steel

# AUSTRALIA
# ASLAV-25 APC/AIFV

*The ASLAV (Australian Light Armoured Vehicle) (Tim Ripley)*

THE CANADIAN/US ARMIES' 8 X 8 LIGHT Armoured Vehicle (LAV-25) has formed the basis of the Australian Light Armoured Vehicle (**ASLAV**) programme. The initial delivery to the Australian Army was for 15 LAV-25s from the US Marine Corps, the vehicles being originally manufactured by Diesel Division, General Motors of Canada and redesignated **ASLAV-25**. In 1992 and 1995 Australia ordered further LAV vehicles, including ASLAV-25s and other ASLAV variants, from the same company, with final fitting being carried out by British Aerospace Australia. In 1999 Tenix Defence Systems took over the British Aerospace Australia's vehicle business, which includes the ASLAV's final fitting. Further orders by the Australian Army are expected, with assembly using some Australian-made components to be carried out in Australia.

The ASLAV-25 has many features in common with later versions of the original Canadian/US LAV-25. The APC/AIFV has a crew of three. The driver is seated in the front left of the hull, with the engine compartment to his right. The commander and gunner are positioned in the two-man power-operated turret mounted towards the rear of the hull, offset to the left. The turret is armed with a Boeing M242 25 mm chain gun, a 7.62 mm MAG 58 coaxial machine-gun and a 7.62 mm MAG 58 anti-aircraft machine-gun on the turret roof. At the rear is the troop compartment, containing six troops seated three each side, back to back. The troop compartment contains six firing ports and vision blocks. The vehicle is fully amphibious, being driven through the water by two propellers at the hull rear. Before entering the water the bilge

pumps are switched on and a trim vane is raised at the front of the hull.

The Australian Army's ASLAV fleet contains a number of variants, including the **ASLAV-PC** (based on the Bison 8 x 8 APC) with a crew of two plus seven troops and armed with a 12.7 mm M2 machine-gun; the **ASLAV-C** command vehicle with a crew of five and extensive radio communications equipment; the **ASLAV-F** fitters' vehicle and the **ASLAV-R** maintenance and recovery vehicle, both of which can be fitted with a winch or a crane; the **ASLAV-S** surveillance vehicle which has a crew of four and carries RASIT ground surveillance radar and other observation equipment, and the **ASLAV-A** ambulance which has a crew of three. All ASLAVs are fitted with a climate-control system and have the option of adding appliqué armour.

## SPECIFICATION:

**Crew:** 3 + 6
**Armament:** 1 x 25 mm gun, 1 x 7.62 mm coaxial machine-gun, 1 x 7.62 mm AA machine-gun, 8 x smoke grenade dischargers
**Ammunition:** 630 rounds, 25 mm; 1,620 rounds, 7.62 mm
**Dimensions:** length 6.39 m
**Weight:** empty 14,243 kg; loaded 16,329 kg
**Engine:** Caterpillar 31268 diesel; output 350 hp
**Performance:** range 500 km; maximum speed 100 km/h
**Armour:** steel

# BMD-3 APC/AIFV

*BMP-3K command vehicle (Tim Ripley)*

THE **BMD-3** AIRBORNE COMBAT VEHICLE was developed in the USSR to follow on from the BMD-1 and BMD-2. Larger and heavier than the previous vehicles, production at the Volgograd Tractor Plant in Russia started in 1989.

The BMD-3 has a basic crew of two, with an additional five troops being accommodated. The driver is seated in the centre of the front of the hull and two other crew members sit either side of the driver. There are three hatches on the front of the hull top. On the left side of the hull a 30 mm AG-17 or 40 mm automatic grenade launcher is mounted and on the right side there is a 5.45 mm RPKS machine-gun. Also mounted on the bow is a 7.62 mm machine-gun. The power-operated turret is the same as that used on the BMP-2 APC/AIFV, and is mounted in the centre behind the front three crew members in the bow, but still in the forward part of the hull. Two men are positioned in the turret, which is armed with a long 30 mm 2A42 cannon, which overhangs the hull, and a coaxial 7.62 mm machine-gun. The roof of the turret also has an ATGW launcher for AT-4 or AT-5 missiles.

The suspension has five tracked road wheels either side, with a hydropneumatic system that enables the vehicle's ground clearance to be adjusted from 0.15 m to 0.53 m, according to the terrain, the normal ground clearance being 0.45 m. The vehicle is also fully amphibious, being propelled in the water by two water jets at the rear of the hull up to a speed of 10 km/h. Before the vehicle enters the water the bilge pumps are switched on and a trim vane is raised at the front of the hull. Options include fitting with wider

480 mm tracks in place of the standard 320 mm-wide tracks. An NBC system and night vision equipment is also fitted.

The BMD-3 is in service only with Russian airborne units, and is still in production. There are no known variants, but the latest Russian APC/AIFV, the BMP-3, which was first seen in 1990, is a likely candidate for similar specialised adaptation as an airborne combat vehicle.

## SPECIFICATION:

**Crew:** 2 + 5
**Armament:** 1 x 30 mm gun, 1 x 7.62 mm coaxial machine-gun, 1 x AT-4 or AT-5 ATGW launcher, 1 x 7.62 mm machine-gun (bow), 1 x 30 mm or 40 mm grenade launcher (bow), 1 x 5.45 mm machine-gun (bow), 6 x smoke grenade launchers
**Ammunition:** 860 rounds, 30 mm; 2,000 rounds, 7.62 mm; 2,160 rounds, 5.45 mm; 551 rounds, 30 mm/40 mm grenades; 4 rounds, ATGW
**Dimensions:** length 6.36 m; height 2.17 m; width 3.13 m; ground clearance 0.15 m–0.53 m
**Weight:** loaded 13,200 kg
**Engine:** 2V-06 water-cooled diesel; output 450 hp
**Performance:** range 500 km; maximum speed 71 km/h; speed cross-country 50 km/h
**Armour:** aluminium

# BMP Family APC/AIFV

*BMP-2 of the Czech Republic Army in Bosnia*

THE USSR PIONEERED THE INTRODUCTION of the mechanised infantry combat vehicle with the introduction of the **BMP-1** into service in 1967. Previously, armoured personnel carriers had been used to convey the mechanised infantry to the location of the action, where they would dismount to fight. The BMP was an advance on this tactic because the infantry could fight from the tracked armoured vehicle, which carried substantial armament with its turreted 73 mm low-pressure smoothbore gun firing HEAT or HE-FRAG (High Explosive Fragmentation) rounds and an AT-3 Sagger ATGW launcher over the 73 mm main armament. The vehicle also has firing ports in the hull through which the infantry section inside can use their rifles or machine-guns in an assault. This firepower enables the momentum of an advance to be increased because it reduces delays as the infantry would otherwise have to dismount frequently. The infantry also have all-round armoured protection compared to the previously used APCs which had open tops, leaving the occupants vulnerable to overhead attack, shell splinters or NBC warfare. Where the infantry have to cover long distances it is crucial they keep up with the tanks when they break through defensive lines, and the increased offensive capability of the

AIFV enables them to do this better than in a relatively lightly armed APC. Also, once dismounted, the BMP can provide effective cover for the attacking infantry. The BMP-1 has an amphibious capability and is fitted with an NBC protection system, and night vision equipment for the crew. The BMP-1 has a crew of three, comprising a driver seated at the front left, a commander located behind the driver and a gunner in the turret. It is able to carry eight infantrymen at the rear, seating four on either side facing outwards. The entrance is via two doors at the rear.

The BMP-1 was followed by the **BMP-2**, which was developed in the late 1970s and first seen by the public in 1982. Being the first of its kind, the design of the BMP-1 proved to have some flaws. Because the commander was seated behind the driver, his visibility was restricted. The BMP-2 is a slightly wider vehicle (although shorter and lower), and the driver is seated front left, with an infantryman to the rear. The larger powered turret fits both the commander and the gunner. However, the revised layout inside means that there is room for only seven infantrymen in the BMP-2, as the rear can accommodate only six sitting three on each side facing outwards. There are four firing ports in the left side of the hull, three in the right and one in the left rear door. As with the BMP-1, the

23

*A BMP-2, armed with a 30 mm cannon, carries a crew of three with seven further troops in the rear compatment*

BMP-2 has night vision equipment and an NBC system. The 73 mm gun on the BMP-1 had also proved to be inaccurate, so this was replaced on the BMP-2 with a 30 mm cannon firing AP-T (Armour Piercing – Tracer) or HE-T (High Explosive – Tracer) rounds, again with a 7.62 mm coaxial machine-gun. The profile of the BMP-2 has a more pronounced sharp prow at the front and longer deflector shroud at the rear. These modifications were introduced to improve the vehicle's amphibious capability. Other modifications include the fitting of the AT-5 Spandrel ATGW, or the shorter-range AT-4 Spigot, both second-generation missiles, as a replacement for the Sagger, and the addition of electrically operated smoke dischargers mounted on both sides of the turret. (Both the BMP-1 and BMP-2 can also lay a smoke screen by injecting diesel fuel into the exhaust outlet on the hull.) Other variations include the BMD, which is an airborne BMP with the same armament, a command post vehicle and the **BMP-R** reconnaissance vehicle.

The BMP-1 and BMP-2 have been sold throughout the world to USSR and Russian clients. As well as being in service with the Russian Army, the BMP-1 has been sold in the past to armed forces in Afghanistan, Algeria, Bulgaria, Cuba, Czechoslovakia, East Germany, Egypt, Ethiopia, Finland, Hungary, India, Iran, Iraq, Libya, Mongolia, North Korea, North Yemen, Poland, Syria and Yugoslavia. It is also built in China as the **Type WZ 501**. Although the BMP had been used with only mixed success in a number of conflicts, such as by the Russians in Chechnya and by Syria in its Middle East wars, many other armed forces, including those in the West, have followed with their own AIFVs. During the Gulf War, the effectiveness of the BMP and other AIFVs on the modern highly mechanised and fast-moving large-scale battlefield was proved beyond doubt.

## SPECIFICATION:

### BMP-1
**Crew:** 3+8
**Armament:** 1 x 73 mm gun, 1 x 7.62 mm coaxial machine-gun, 1 x AT-3 Sagger anti-tank missile launcher
**Ammunition:** 40 rounds, 73 mm; 2,000 rounds, 7.62 mm; 5 rounds, AT-3 Sagger
**Dimensions:** length 6.74 m; height 2.15 m; width 2.94 m; ground clearance 0.39 m
**Weight:** empty 12,500 kg; loaded 13,500 kg; ground pressure 0.6 kg/cm²
**Engine:** Type 5D20 6-cylinder inline water-cooled diesel; output 300 hp
**Performance:** range 500 km; maximum speed 65 km/h; speed cross-country n/a
**Armour:** steel – 33 mm max.

### BMP-2
**Crew:** 3+7
**Armament:** 1 x 30 mm gun, 1 x 7.62 mm coaxial machine-gun, 1 x AT-5 Spandrel or AT-4 Spigot anti-tank missile launcher, 6 x smoke dischargers
**Ammunition:** 500 rounds, 30 mm; 2,000 rounds, 7.62 mm; 4 rounds, Spandrel ATGW
**Dimensions:** length 6.71 m; height 2.06 m; width 3.09 m; ground clearance 0.42 m
**Weight:** loaded 14,600 kg; ground pressure 0.64 kg/cm²
**Engine:** 6-cylinder supercharged diesel; output 400 hp
**Performance:** range 600 km; maximum speed 65 km/h; speed cross-country n/a
**Armour:** steel – 33 mm max.

# BMP-3 APC/AIFV

FIRST SEEN IN 1990, THE **BMP-3** IS THE LATEST in the line of APC/AIFVs developed for the Russian Army. As with the BMP-1 and BMP-2, the vehicle has a three-man crew. The driver sits at the front centre of the vehicle with an infantryman either side of him. As with the BMP-2, the turret accommodates two crew and is positioned in the centre of the large box-type hull. The commander sits on the right of the turret and the gunner on the left. The engine compartment is at the rear right of the vehicle, the fuel tanks being carried beneath the floor. There is a small troop compartment also at the rear of the BMP-3 which is accessed via two small outward-opening doors in the hull rear with steps that unfold down to the ground, necessitated by the high floor of the compartment. The troop compartment also has hatches in the roof; overall there is room for seven troops in the vehicle, with the troop compartment carrying five. The vehicle is fitted with NBC and night vision equipment for the crew.

The 100 mm rifled main gun is mounted on the turret and can fire both conventional ammunition and a laser-guided ATGW designated as AAT-10 by NATO. To the right on the turret is a 30 mm cannon which is attached to the main gun. One 7.62 mm machine-gun is coaxially mounted further to the right, while another two 7.62 mm machine-guns are mounted on each side of the hull front, firing forwards.

Each side of the suspension has six road wheels and the upper part of the track is covered by a light steel cover. The suspension can also be adjusted by the driver according to the type of terrain being covered. The vehicle is fully amphibious, being propelled through the water by two water jets mounted at the rear of the hull.

The BMP-3 is still in production at the Kurgan Machine Construction Plant, Russia, and is in service

*The BMP-3 of the United Arab Emirates in Kosovo as part of the KFOR force (VS-Books Carl Schulze)*

with the Russian Army, as well as in Azerbaijan, Cyprus, Kuwait, South Korea, Ukraine and the United Arab Emirates. There are a number of variants, including a reconnaissance vehicle (**BRM** or **Rys** [Lynx]), a recovery vehicle (**BREM-L**), a driver training vehicle and a command vehicle (**BMP-3K**). The **BMP-3M** is the latest export model and there are two ATGW prototypes – the **BMP-3 Kornet** and **BMP-3 Krizantema**. The BMP-3 chassis is also the basis of the 120 mm 2S31 Vena artillery system.

---

## SPECIFICATION:

**Crew:** 3+7

**Armament:** 1 x 100 mm, 1 x 30 mm coaxial gun, 1 x 7.62 mm coaxial machine-gun, 2 x 7.62 mm machine-guns, 6 x smoke dischargers

**Ammunition:** 40 rounds, 100 mm; 500 rounds, 30 mm; 6,000 rounds, 7.62 mm; 6 x ATGWs

**Dimensions:** length 7.14 m; height (turret roof) 2.30 m; width 3.15 m; ground clearance 0.51 m (adjustable)

**Weight:** loaded 18,700 kg; ground pressure 0.61 kg/cm²

**Engine:** diesel; output 500 hp

**Performance:** range 600 km; maximum speed 70 km/h; speed cross-country 50 km/h

**Armour:** steel

# BRDM-2

*The BRDM-2 four-wheel-drive scout car (Tim Ripley)*

THE **BRDM** HAS BEEN THE BACKBONE of Russian ground reconnaissance since the **BRDM-1** 4 x 4 amphibious scout car was introduced in the late 1950s. The USSR armed forces needed a mobile amphibious vehicle as its predecessors had been unable to keep up with their amphibious PT-76 reconnaissance tank also developed in the 1950s. However, although successful, the USSR armed forces decided in the 1960s that they needed to improve the BRDM-1, and developed the **BRDM-2**, which came into service in 1966. The improvements included a one-man turret armed with 14.5 mm and 7.62 mm machine-guns, with the crew compartment moved forward, and a more powerful 140 hp engine was moved to the rear, increasing the performance on land and in the water. Although heavier, it had an improved top speed of 100 km/h, with a speed of 10 km/h through the water, and its range was increased from 500 km to 750 km. The 4 x 4 BRDM-2 has the facility when travelling cross-country of lowering an extra pair of belly wheels to give added mobility. It is propelled in the water by a single water jet mounted at the rear of the hull. The vehicle is equipped with infra-red night vision and an NBC system.

The BRDM-2 has been sold widely around the world. The old Warsaw Pact countries such as Bulgaria, East Germany, Hungary, Poland and Romania took a number, and many others have been sold throughout the world, including to many countries in the Third World. Among the 50-plus customers worldwide have been Algeria, Ethiopia, India, Iraq, Israel, Morocco, Nicaragua, Peru, Sudan, Syria, Tanzania, Yugoslavia, Zambia and Zimbabwe. The BRDM-2's versatile design, with its simple controls and ease of handling, has meant that is has been adapted to many roles, including a command

vehicle with an extra generator to power the increased number of radios, a chemical reconnaissance vehicle with lane-marking equipment at the rear, a chemical decontamination vehicle, and an air defence (the SA-9 Gaskin) variant. There have also been a number of anti-tank versions giving reconnaissance units a long-range anti-tank capability. These carry ready-to-launch missiles on a launching rail or traverser which opens at the hull rear, and the latest, the **BRDM-3**, carries five AT-3 Spandrel missiles in their launchers, with extra missiles carried inside for manual loading. The Hungarians have also produced a version of the BRDM-2 which was slightly modified for their requirements, called the FUG, which was also sold to Czechoslovakia.

## SPECIFICATION:

**Crew:** 4
**Armament:** 1 x 14.5 mm machine-gun, 1 x 7.62 mm coaxial machine-gun
**Ammunition:** 500 rounds, 14.5 mm; 2,000 rounds, 7.62 mm
**Dimensions:** length 5.75 m; height 2.31 m; width 2.35 m; ground clearance 0.43 m
**Weight:** loaded 7,000 kg; ground pressure n/a
**Engine:** GAZ-41 V-8 water-cooled petrol; output 140 hp
**Performance:** range 750 km; maximum speed 100 km/h; speed cross-country n/a
**Armour:** steel – 14 mm

## RUSSIA
# BTR-90 APC/AIFV

THE HIGHLY SUCCESSFUL RUSSIAN BTR series of 8 x 8 armoured personnel carriers has been in service since the BTR-60 was first seen in public in 1961. The BTR-60 was first redeveloped as the BTR-70 in the late 1970s and then as the BTR-80 in the early 1980s. Although all three types of BTR are still in service in many countries throughout the world and the BTR-80 is still in production, by the 1990s the Russian Army decided it needed a further upgraded BTR. Design of the new 8 x 8 vehicle, the **BTR-90** (also called the **Obiekt 51** or **GAZ-5923**), started in 1993, and the first prototype was exhibited in 1994. The vehicle is now in production, being manufactured by the Arzamas Machinery Construction Plant, which also produces the BTR-80, although the hull is built at the Chelyabinsk Factory for Heavy Machinery Construction and the diesel engine is supplied by the Chelyabinsk Tractor Factory. There are no known variants.

Although very similar to the BTR-80, the BTR-90 has some important differences. The all-welded steel hull with its slightly V-shaped bottom gives better protection against mines, as well as small-arms fire and shell splinters. The armament has also been upgraded, with the complete turret of the BMP-2 AIFV being mounted on the BTR-90. The turret is armed with a stabilised 30 mm 2A42 cannon, a 7.62 mm coaxial PKT machine-gun and a roof-mounted AT-5 Spandrel ATGW system. Latest versions of the BTR-90 also have a 30 mm AGS-17 grenade launcher mounted externally on the turret. The three-man crew of the BTR-90 comprises the driver seated at the front of the hull on the left with an infantryman to his right, and the commander seated on the right of the turret in the centre of the hull, with the gunner to his left. Behind the turret the troop compartment can carry eight to ten infantrymen, while the engine compartment is at the rear of the

*BTR-90 APC with 30 mm cannon as main armament and 30 mm automatic grenade launcher on turret side*

hull. Access for all crew members and infantry is via a two-piece door, the lower half of which folds down to form a ramp, between the second and third wheels or roof hatches. The infantry can fire through roof hatches or firing ports in the troop compartment. The vehicle is fully amphibious, being propelled through the water by two water jets at the rear of the hull. Standard equipment includes an array of periscopes above the driver's and troop compartments and the turret, passive night vision equipment, an NBC system, central tyre-pressure regulation and power-assisted steering for the front four wheels.

---

## SPECIFICATION:

**Crew:** 3 + 7

**Armament:** 1 x 30 mm main gun, 1 x 7.62 mm coaxial machine-gun, 1 x AT-5 Spandrel ATGW, 1 x 30 mm grenade launcher, 6 x smoke grenade dischargers

**Ammunition:** 500 rounds, 30 mm; 2,000 rounds, 7.62 mm, 4 rounds, AT-5 Spandrel ATGW; 400 rounds, 30 mm grenades

**Dimensions:** length 7.64 m; height 2.98 m; width 3.20 m; ground clearance 0.51 m

**Weight:** loaded 20,920 kg

**Engine:** turbo-charged multi-fuel; output 510 hp

**Performance:** range 800 km; maximum speed 100 km/h

**Armour:** steel

# BTR-T APC/AIFV

*The BTR-T Heavy Armoured Personnel Carrier*
*(Military Parade Magazine)*

THE **BTR-T** HEAVY ARMOURED PERSONNEL carrier has been developed using the chassis of the T-54/T-55 MBT to improve the protection of Russian infantry when operating alongside heavy armour. The BTR-T was first seen in public in 1997 and is manufactured by the GUP Design Bureau of Transport Machine Building, although it is still at only the prototype stage.

The use of the T-54/T-55 MBT chassis means that the BTR-T can be constructed at a relatively low cost. The original turret has been removed from the chassis and the hull raised to accommodate the crew at the front and the troop compartment at the rear. The engine compartment is kept at the rear of the hull. The crew comprises the driver seated front left and the commander/gunner seated in the turret. Up to five infantrymen can be carried in the troop compartment. Access for the crew and infantry is solely via hatches situated to the front and rear of the turret, with the infantry at the rear being able to survey outside using observation periscopes in the troop compartment.

A new turret has been fitted to the front left of the hull. The turret is of a modular design, allowing a range of either Russian-built or Western weapons to be fitted, but it is believed that the standard armament consists of a 30 mm 2A42 automatic cannon and a pintle-mounted Konkurs (AT-5 Spandrel) anti-tank guided missile launcher fixed below, to the right. Other possible variations of armament include the prototype BMP-3 turret with 30 mm cannon, 30 mm grenade launcher and 7.62 mm machine-gun; 30 mm cannon and twin-round AT-5 Spandrel launcher; 30 mm cannon with 30 mm grenade

launcher; twin 30 mm cannon; 12.7 mm machine-gun and twin-round AT-5 Spandrel launcher; and 12.7 mm machine-gun and 30 mm grenade launcher. Potentially, it is thought that the BTR-T could even be built using the chassis of Western MBTs. The BTR-T also has four banks of three forward-firing smoke dischargers on the rear of the hull, and can lay a smokescreen by injecting diesel into the exhaust. The original T-54/T-55 chassis has also been given extra ERA armour protection on the BTR-T, similar to that used on the T-80U-series MBTs, to provide improved protection against both kinetic and chemical attack.

## SPECIFICATION:

**Crew:** 2 + 5
**Armament:** 1 x 30 mm main gun, 1 x AT-5 Spandrel ATGW launcher
**Ammunition:** n/a
**Weight:** loaded 38,500 kg
**Engine:** (T-54/55) V-12 water-cooled diesel; output 520 hp
**Performance:** maximum speed 50 km/h; speed cross-country n/a
**Armour:** steel

# BTR-70 and 80 APC/AIFV

THE BTR SERIES OF ARMOURED PERSONNEL carriers has been developed over many years from the original BTR-60 family of 8 x 8 APCs which entered service with the USSR Army in 1960. The **BTR-70**, which was developed from the BTR-60 and was first seen in the USSR in 1980, had a number of improvements compared to its predecessor: better armour protection at the front, a more powerful engine giving an improved power-to-weight ratio and better visibility from the troop compartment with extra firing ports. The BTR-70 is fitted with the same manual turret as the BTR-60PB, on which is mounted a 14.5 mm and a 7.62 mm coaxial machine-gun. The vehicle has a crew of two, with the commander and driver seated together at the front. Behind them is the troop compartment which can carry nine soldiers. As with the BTR-60, there are two petrol engines at the rear: one drives the four wheels on one side of the chassis, the other the four wheels on the other side. It is also fitted with a central tyre-pressure-regulation system for rough terrain. The vehicle is also fully amphibious, being propelled through the water by a single water jet at the rear of the hull. There are a number of variants, including a command vehicle (**BTR-70KShM**), a communications vehicle without turret (**BTR-70MS**) and a chemical reconnaissance vehicle (**BTR-70Kh**). It is believed that there is also a radar-jamming variant (**SPR-2**). BTR-70s have also been fitted with roof-mounted grenade launchers and, recently, the BTR-80's turret. The manufacturer, the Gorki Automobile Plant, Russia, has ceased production of the BTR-70, but the vehicle is still in service in the Russian Army and has been used in the conflicts in Afghanistan, Chechnya and the Gulf War. It is also in service in Afghanistan, Hungary, Macedonia, Pakistan and a number of former USSR republics.

The **BTR-80**, which entered service in the mid-1980s, was a further improvement, as its design allowed better access to the rear troop compartment and had a more powerful single V-8 diesel engine. The turret is similar to that on the BTR-70, retaining the same 14.5 mm and 7.62 mm machine-gun armament, but the 14.5 mm machine-gun can be elevated higher to act as an AA gun. Six smoke grenade launchers have also been added to the turret rear. The BTR-80 carries three crew and seven troops in the rear compartment, which has firing ports. Access to the troop compartment has been improved by the addition of a hatch between the second and third axles, with a step down to the ground. The BTR-80

*A Romanian BTR-70 of the Implementation Force in Bosnia*

has the same amphibious facility as the BTR-70. Variants include a command vehicle (**BTR-80 M1989/1**), the **BTR-80A** with a new turret with 30 mm cannon and 7.62 mm machine-gun and the **RKhM-4** chemical and reconnaissance vehicle. The BTR-80 chassis has also been used for the 120 mm 2S23 SP artillery. The BTR-80 is still in production, being manufactured by Arzamas Machinery Construction Plant, Russia, and is in service in Afghanistan, Bangladesh, Finland, Hungary, Turkey and South Korea, as well as with the armed forces in Russia and other former USSR republics.

## SPECIFICATION:

**BTR-70**
**Crew:** 2+9
**Armament:** 1 x 14.5 mm machine-gun, 1 x 7.62 mm coaxial machine-gun
**Ammunition:** 500 rounds, 14.5 mm; 2,000 rounds, 7.62 mm
**Dimensions:** length 7.54 m; height 2.32 m; width 2.80 m; ground clearance 0.48 m
**Weight:** loaded 11,500 kg
**Engine:** 2 x ZMZ-4905 6-cylinder petrol; output 115 hp each
**Performance:** range 600 km; maximum speed 80 km/h
**Armour:** steel – 9 mm max.

**BTR-80**
**Crew:** 3+7
**Armament:** 1 x 14.5 mm machine-gun, 1 x 7.62 mm coaxial machine-gun, 6 x smoke grenade launchers
**Ammunition:** 500 rounds, 14.5 mm; 2,000 rounds, 7.62 mm
**Dimensions:** length 7.65 m; height 2.35 m; width 2.90 m; ground clearance 0.48 m
**Weight:** loaded 13,600 kg
**Engine:** 4-stroke V-8 water-cooled diesel; output 260 hp
**Performance:** range 600 km; maximum speed 90 km/h
**Armour:** steel – 9 mm max.

*BTR-80 of the Russian Guards Division*

# Casspir APC/AIFV Mine Protected Vehicles

THE **CASSPIR** FAMILY OF ARMOURED personnel carriers started development in South Africa in the late 1970s, the first vehicles being manufactured by TFM. The success of the early Casspir meant that the **Mk II** and today the **Mk III** have been developed, although they are now manufactured by Reumech OMC, in Benoni, South Africa, as this company has now taken TFM over.

The distinctive V-shaped hull of the Casspir is raised high off the ground. These features protect the crew against anti-tank mines as they help to deflect the blast and reduce its effects. The large wheels and 4 x 4 configuration mean that the vehicle can easily travel cross-country. The Casspir has a crew of two and can carry an additional ten personnel. The commander and driver are positioned immediately behind the engine compartment, which is housed in the bonnet at the front of the vehicle. The troop compartment extends from behind the crew to the back of the vehicle and seats five troops on each side, facing inwards. Early versions have an open roof to the troop compartment but later versions have an enclosed troop compartment, with access being through twin doors at the rear of the hull. The windows at the front of the vehicle and along the sides of the troop compartment are bullet-proof, with those towards the rear of the vehicle also having firing ports below them. Although there are some minor changes between different Casspir models, there are a number of standard features, including a long-range fuel tank, two spare wheels and tyres mounted on either side of the chassis rear, fire extinguishers and a tank of drinking water. The vehicle is armed with up to three 7.62 mm machine-guns, one of which is

*Casspir APC of the South African police force*

usually mounted on the hull top at the front, which is armoured, and can also carry a rubber bullet launcher. Optional extras include floodlights, searchlights and obstacle-clearing equipment.

The Casspir Mk III is in service with the South African armed forces, who have used it for internal security as well as in other conflicts in Southern Africa. It has also been sold to Angola, India, Namibia, Peru and Uganda. Variants include mine-clearing and sensor vehicles, an artillery control vehicle, the **Gemsbok**, which has recovery equipment fitted to the rear of the hull and an extended armoured cab, the **Duiker** 5,000-litre fuel tanker, the **Blesbok** cargo carrier and ambulance and police vehicles.

---

## SPECIFICATION:

**Crew:** 2+10
**Armament:** up to 3 x 7.62 mm machine-guns
**Dimensions:** length 6.87 m; height 2.85 m; width 2.5 m; ground clearance (axle) 0.41 m
**Weight:** empty 11,040 kg; loaded 12,580 kg
**Engine:** AADE-352T 6-cylinder diesel; output 170 hp
**Performance:** range 850 km; maximum speed 90 km/h
**Armour:** steel

# Centauro Light Tank/Recce Vehicle

*Centauro 8 x 8 tank destroyer*

THE **CENTAURO** IS AN ARMOURED 8 X 8 vehicle developed as a tank destroyer for the Italian Army following successful trials of the APC prototype. The first deliveries took place in 1991, the manufacturing being split between Otobreda at La Spezia, Italy, which supplies the turret, including the armament, and Iveco at Bolzano, Italy, which produces the hull. The Centauro carries a crew of four. The driver is seated in the front left of the vehicle, with the engine compartment on his right. Behind are the commander, gunner and loader in the power-operated turret which is mounted towards the rear of the vehicle. The armament carried on the turret consists of a large 105 mm gun, the barrel of which overhangs the front of the hull and has a muzzle brake, a thermal sleeve and fume extractor, one coaxial 7.62 mm gun, one anti-aircraft 7.62 mm machine-gun and eight smoke grenade dischargers. The commander and gunner are seated on the right and the loader on the left of the turret. Access for the crew is either via two roof hatches or through a hatch in the rear, which is also used to load ammunition. The Centauro is part of the new family of armoured vehicles manufactured by Iveco and Otobreda in service with the Italian Army (e.g. the Ariete main battle tank, the Dardo infantry fighting vehicle and the Puma 4 x 4 and 6 x 6 armoured personnel car), and uses a similar computerised fire control system to that fitted in the Ariete, with night vision equipment. The hydropneumatic suspension has four large road wheels on either side, with power-assisted steering for the front two wheels on each side. The vehicle also has a central tyre-pressure-regulation system so that the ground pressure can be adjusted according to the terrain being crossed. Other systems fitted include an NBC system and a fire detection and suppression system.

The Centauro is in service only with the Italian Army, and has been used as part of the United Nations forces in recent conflicts in the former Yugoslav republics, for which it has had additional armour fitted. Production of the Centauro has now finished, as the Italian Army's order for 400 vehicles has now been fulfilled. There are no variants, although an armoured recovery vehicle and a 155 mm self-propelled gun have been projected.

## SPECIFICATION:

**Crew:** 4
**Armament:** 1 x 105 mm gun, 1 x 7.62 mm coaxial machine-gun, 1 x 7.62 mm AA machine-gun, 8 x smoke dischargers
**Ammunition:** 40 rounds, 105 mm; 4,000 rounds, 7.62 mm
**Dimensions:** length (with gun) 8.56 m, (hull) 7.85 m; height 2.74 m; width 3.05 m; ground clearance 0.42 m
**Weight:** loaded 25,000 kg
**Engine:** Iveco Fiat MTCA V-6 turbo-charged diesel; output 520 hp
**Performance:** range 800 km; maximum speed 105 km/h
**Armour:** steel

# Centurion Olifant MBT and Technology Demonstrator

*Centurion Olifant MBT of the South African Army*

THE HIGHLY SUCCESSFUL AND LONG-LIVED Centurion main battle tank series, originally developed for the British Army at the end of World War II, was sold to South Africa along with many other countries in over 30 years of production. The first Centurions exported to South Africa were Mk 3 models in 1953, which were upgraded to Mk 5, and over the years Centurions were also bought second-hand from a number of countries, including Jordan. By the 1970s the United Nations' embargo on the sale of military equipment to South Africa led to the South Africans deciding to upgrade their increasingly outdated Centurion main battle tank force. The extensive modernisation of their Centurions was started in the early 1970s, the first conversions fitting the Centurions with a new V-12 petrol engine in a project called Skokiaan, followed by some improved Centurions called Mk 5A or Semel being fitted with a modified engine. The first prototype **Olifant Mk 1** (elephant) was produced in 1976 by OMC Engineering (Pty) Ltd at the 61 Basis Werksplaas (61 Base Workshops) in Verwoerdburg. (The company subsequently became Reumech OMC and then Vickers Reumech in 1999.) The Mk 1 Olifant was basically a Centurion with a modified engine, suspension, turret drive and vision equipment, and the Olifant was further upgraded when development on the **Mk 1A** started in 1983, with the first vehicles being delivered in 1985. The Mk 1A Olifant replaced the Centurion's original Rolls-Royce Meteor Mk IVB 12-cylinder liquid-cooled petrol engine, which had

proved uneconomical and required frequent maintenance, with a more efficient air-cooled V-12 diesel engine. The South Africans also designed for the Mk 1A Olifant their own version of the highly successful British L7 105 mm rifled main gun. Early versions of the Centurion had been fitted first with a 17-pounder (76.2 mm), and subsequently with a 20-pounder (83.8 mm) main gun, but the British Army versions from the Mk 5 in the late 1950s onwards were fitted with the L7-series 105 mm gun, as well as a 7.62 mm coaxial machine-gun and another 7.62 mm anti-aircraft machine-gun. The L7 has proved to be an extremely accurate and consistent gun and the design has been adopted as a standard in many Western countries. Passive night vision equipment was also installed, new sights and a laser range-finder provided for the commander and gunner and a new commander's cupola fitted.

The Mk 1A Olifant has subsequently been extensively rebuilt as the **Olifant Mk 1B**, the first prototype being completed in 1985 and the first production vehicles being delivered in 1991. The Olifant Mk 1B rebuild has been given a new, more powerful, V-12 diesel engine and new transmission. The bogie-type suspension in the Mk 1A has been replaced by torsion bars and the hull floor strengthened by torsion bars inserted between double floor plates, providing added protection against mines. Elsewhere the armour has been upgraded, with appliqué armour added to the glacis plate, forward hull and turret, and modular side skirts fitted to

protect the suspension. New electronic instrument panels, night vision devices, sighting devices including periscopes, searchlights and laser rangefinders are provided for the crew of four (the driver, gunner, loader and commander). The 105 mm main gun is now fitted with a thermal sleeve and fume extractor, and a fire-detection/suppression system has also been installed. The main visible changes are the fitting of a turret bustle for increased stowage and the addition of a new driver's hatch and escape hatch to the hull. The Olifant Mk 1B can also be fitted with a V-shaped bar at the front to help the vehicle push its way through thick vegetation.

A prototype new turret for the Olifant, called the Olifant 2, has also recently been produced by LIW Division of Denel. The distinctive arrowhead-shaped turret can be armed with either the LIW 105 mm GT-8 rifled tank gun or the LIW 120 mm smooth-bore gun, as well having a 7.62 mm coaxial machine-gun and banks of smoke grenade dischargers. The turret crew comprises a gunner seated on the right, a commander seated behind and a loader/gunner on the left. A high level of protection is provided by the modular armour added to the all-welded steel hull, with blow-off panels fitted inside the turret roof to reduce the potential danger of the ammunition exploding when it is stored either in the turret bustle or ready to use in the turret basket. The Olifant 2 turret is fitted with the latest fire-control system, and thermal imaging and night vision sighting systems.

The Olifant is in service only with the South African Defence Force and has seen combat service in the conflict in Angola. Variants include a mine-clearing vehicle, an armoured recovery vehicle and an armoured-vehicle-launched bridge.

## SPECIFICATION:

### Olifant Mk 1A
**Crew:** 4
**Armament:** 1 x 105 mm main gun, 1 x 7.62 mm coaxial machine-gun, 1 x 7.62 mm AA machine-gun, 8 x 81 mm smoke grenade dischargers
**Ammunition:** 72 rounds, 105 mm; 5,600 rounds, 7.62 mm
**Dimensions:** length 8.29 m; height 2.94 m; width 3.39 m
**Weight:** loaded 56,000 kg
**Engine:** V-12 diesel; output 750 hp
**Performance:** range 500 km; maximum speed 45 km/h
**Armour:** steel

### Olifant Mk 1B
**Crew:** 4
**Armament:** 1 x 105 mm main gun, 1 x 7.62 mm coaxial machine-gun, 1 x 7.62 mm AA machine-gun, 8 x 81 mm smoke grenade dischargers
**Ammunition:** 68 rounds, 105 mm; 5,000 rounds, 7.62 mm
**Dimensions:** length 8.61 m; height 3.55 m; width 3.42 m; ground clearance 0.35 m
**Weight:** loaded 58,000 kg
**Engine:** V-12 diesel; output 950 hp
**Performance:** range 500 km; maximum speed 58 km/h
**Armour:** steel and composite passive armour

# Challenger 2 and 2E MBT

*Vickers Defence Systems Challenger 2 (Tim Ripley)*

**A**LTHOUGH ORIGINALLY DEVELOPED privately by Vickers Defence Systems based in Leeds, UK, the **Challenger 2** has become the latest main battle tank to be used by the British Army, replacing both the Chieftain, which first entered service with the British Army in 1967, and the Challenger 1, the Challenger 2's immediate predecessor, which entered service in 1983, with the last deliveries being made in the early 1990s. Although less mobile than the other MBTs of its generation, the Chieftain was extremely effective, being one of the most heavily armoured, with one of the largest main guns (120 mm), but by the late 1960s and 1970s the British Army was looking towards the next generation of MBTs. Challenger 1 evolved from the Chieftain, being based on an MBT that Vickers was developing for Iran, called Shir 1. Although the Iranian order fell through, the Challenger was then developed for the British Army from the Shir 2 prototype, with production starting in 1978. The Challenger 1 was not regarded as entirely satisfactory, and although performing well in Operation 'Desert Storm' during the Gulf War in 1991, there were doubts about the effectiveness of its armament evinced by an earlier withdrawal from the NATO tank contest, the Canadian Army Trophy. It was decided in the late 1980s that the British Army needed to find a new MBT, and after a series of rigorous tests were agreed the design of the Challenger 2 was chosen ahead of

the German Leopard 2 (Improved), the French Leclerc and the US M1A1 Abrams.

Initially the Challenger 2 was intended to supersede only half of the Challenger 1 fleet, as well as the remaining Chieftains in the British Army, but it was subsequently decided to replace them all. Nine prototypes were built by Vickers, and following a successful demonstration phase the British Army signed a production contract in 1991, the tank being formally accepted in 1994, when the first of the total order of 386 MBTs was produced. Although Challenger 2 is fundamentally a new MBT, there are similarities to the Challenger 1, chiefly in the design of the hull. The driver sits centrally at the front, with an unusual depression in the glacis plate in front of him to enable him to see. The remaining three crew members are in the turret: the commander and gunner are positioned to the right of the main gun and the loader to the left. The gunner's sight is on the right side of the turret roof and there is a raised periscope sight in front of the commander's cupola. For safety, charges are stored in armoured boxes below the turret ring. The turret is an entirely new design constructed from second-generation Chobham armour and welded steel (as is the hull), giving good protection against both kinetic and chemical attack, on which is mounted the new Royal Ordnance L30A1 120 mm rifled main gun. The rifled barrel is less common today than the smooth-bore, but enables

*The Challenger 2E has been designed with desert use in mind (Tim Ripley)*

HESH (High Explosive Squash Head) rounds to be fired as well as the more conventional APFSDS and APDS rounds. The L30A1 is chrome-plated and is fitted with a thermal sleeve, a fume extractor and a muzzle reference system. The gun is fully electrically stabilised and the turret traverse through the full 360 degrees and gun elevation from −10 degrees to +20 degrees is also all-electric. The additional armament on the turret comprises a 7.62 mm coaxial machine-gun to the left of the main gun, and a second, anti-aircraft, 7.62 mm machine-gun mounted on the turret roof, as well as ten smoke grenade launchers. The overall Challenger armament (known as CHARM) package includes the main gun, a new charge system and a new anti-tank round which uses a depleted uranium (DU) penetrator. The engine compartment for the Perkins Condor V-12 12-cylinder diesel engine is at the rear of the hull, slightly raised. The TN54 transmission, with six forward gears and two reverse, is regarded as more flexible than the TN37 model used by the Challenger 1. Night vision equipment and an NBC system are also fitted as standard.

A new version, the **Challenger 2E** (originally known as the **Desert Challenger**), has been designed for desert use and is being offered for export, chiefly to the Middle East. Its modifications include a German MTU diesel engine, increased fuel capacity, a steering wheel in place of the standard tillers and a 12.7 mm machine-gun on the turret roof

instead of the Challenger 2's 7.62 mm anti-aircraft machine-gun. To cope with the high temperatures it has improved airflow in the engine compartment and air conditioning. There are no other variants (except driver training vehicles), and apart from the British Army the only other country to order the Challenger 2 has been Oman.

## SPECIFICATION:

**Challenger 2**
**Crew:** 4
**Armament:** 1 x 120 mm gun, 1 x 7.62 mm coaxial machine-gun, 1 x 7.62 mm anti-aircraft gun, 10 x smoke grenade launchers
**Ammunition:** 50 rounds, 120 mm; 4,000 rounds, 7.62 mm
**Dimensions:** length (gun forwards) 11.55 m, (hull) 8.33 m; height 2.49 m; width 3.52 m; ground clearance 0.50 m
**Weight:** loaded 62,500 kg; ground pressure 0.9 kg/cm$^2$
**Engine:** Perkins CV-12 Condor V-12 12-cylinder diesel; output 1,200 hp
**Performance:** range 450 km; maximum speed 56 km/h
**Armour:** Chobham second-generation/steel

# Challenger CRARRV

*The Challenger CRARRV (Tim Ripley)*

ALTHOUGH THE CHALLENGER 1 MBT is being phased out of the British Army, being replaced by the Challenger 2, the only variant produced – the Challenger Armoured Repair and Recovery Vehicle – is still in service. Development of the **CRARRV** was started in 1985 by Vickers Defence Systems, Newcastle-upon-Tyne, UK, with the first prototypes being completed in 1987. A total of 81 CRARRVs were ordered by the British Army from Vickers, production being carried out at two sites – Leeds and Newcastle-upon-Tyne. The first production vehicles were delivered from each site in 1990 in time for 12 of the vehicles to be used in Operation 'Desert Storm' against the Iraqi Army in 1991. The CRARRV performed extremely well in the difficult desert conditions, suffering no mechanical breakdowns.

The CRARRV carries a crew of three, with additional space for two fitters if required. The vehicle is fitted with a range of specialised equipment, including a Rotzler 52-tonne hydraulic winch, an additional auxiliary winch, an Atlas hydraulically operated crane able to lift a complete Challenger 1 or 2 MBT power-pack and a front-mounted multi-purpose dozer blade which can be used for clearing obstacles as well as acting as an earth anchor or stabiliser for the crane. The engine in the CRARRV is the standard Challenger 1 and 2 MBT Rolls-Royce Perkins CV-12 diesel engine which develops 1,200 hp, although, unlike the Challenger 1 MBT, the CRARRV is fitted with the more flexible TN54 transmission also fitted to the Challenger 2 MBT, which has six forward and two reverse gears. As with the Challenger 1 and

2 MBTs, the hull of the CRARRV has Chobham armour in the hull which gives a high level of protection against both kinetic and chemical energy attack.

The CRARRV is in service with the British Army and has been sold abroad to Oman. A new variant of the CRARRV has also been ordered by the British Army to replace its remaining Chieftain ARVs. The vehicle, called the **Heavy Armoured Repair and Recovery Vehicle**, will be produced at Vickers' Newcastle-upon-Tyne site, and it is intended that it will enter service in 2003.

## SPECIFICATION:

**Crew:** 3 + 2
**Armament:** 7.62 mm machine-gun
**Ammunition:** 1,000 rounds
**Dimensions:** length 9.61 m; height 3.13 m; width 3.62 m; ground clearance 0.90 m
**Weight:** loaded 61,200 kg
**Engine:** Perkins Engine Company Condor CV-12 diesel; output 1,200 hp
**Performance:** range 450 km; maximum speed 56 km/h; speed cross-country 40 km/h
**Armour:** steel

# Chieftain AVRE/ARRV/AVLB

*Chieftain AVLB with No. 8 tank bridge and full width mine-clearing plough*

**Chieftain Armoured Repair and Recovery Vehicle**

DESIGNED IN THE 1950s BY THE BRITISH ARMY to supersede its Centurion MBT, the **Chieftain** MBT was one of the most successful postwar tank designs, being in service for almost 30 years in the British Army as well as being sold throughout the world. The rugged tank, built by the Royal Ordnance at Leeds and Vickers-Armstrong, Elswick, UK (taken over by Vickers Defence Systems in 1986), was characterised by its heavy steel armour protection (with Stillbrew appliqué armour fitted to later British Army models) and large 120 mm main gun, albeit at the cost of some mobility when compared to its rivals. Although the Chieftain main battle tank was phased out of the British Army in 1996, the **ARV** (Armoured Recovery Vehicle), **AVLB** (Armoured Vehicle-Launched Bridge) and **AVRE** (Armoured Vehicle Royal Engineers) are still in service.

The Chieftain ARV, manufactured by Vickers at Elswick, is based on the hull of the Chieftain Mk 5,

and is equipped with the full range of equipment for the recovery of abandoned or disabled vehicles, including a hydraulically operated earth anchor mounted on the front of the hull, a main winch and an auxiliary winch, both hydraulically operated. The ARV is operated by a crew of four, and is armed with a cupola-mounted 7.62 mm machine-gun and 66 mm smoke grenade dischargers. There is also an **ARRV** variant fitted with a hydraulic crane. The Chieftain ARV has also been sold to Iran and Jordan.

The Chieftain Mk 6 AVLB was produced by Vickers Defence Systems in 1986 by converting Chieftain Mk 1/4 MBTs. The turret was replaced with an armoured roof plate with a commander's hatch and the bridge-launching mechanism installed on the roof plate and modified hull. Chobham armour was also fitted to the hull to provide extra protection, and the driver's and crew compartments were refitted. The AVLB carries either a folding No. 8 bridge on the front

*Chieftain ARRV showing hydraulic lifting crane*

*Chieftain MBT with Stillbrew armour*

of its hull, which can span over 22 m using hydraulic power controlled from within the hull and can be uncoupled and recovered later, or a No. 9 bridge which is carried horizontally and swung vertically round to be laid in front, spanning over 12 m. A mine-clearing plough can also be mounted at the front, and a trailer carrying a Royal Ordnance Giant Viper mine-clearing system towed at the back. The AVLB was used in the Gulf War and has been sold to Iran. A new Close Support Bridge (CSB) system consisting of three new tank-launched bridges, modified Chieftain AVLBs and a tank bridge transporter (TBT) truck is currently being developed by Vickers to replace the Chieftain AVLB.

The initial Chieftain AVREs were converted from Chieftain MBTs at the Army Engineer Workshops at Willich in West Germany in 1986, but in 1989 Vickers Defence Systems at Newcastle-upon-Tyne, UK, started developing a new AVRE, again by converting Chieftains. The first prototypes were completed in 1991, and production continued at Vickers' Leeds site until 1994. The new AVREs were given a new superstructure, a 10-tonne winch fixed to the hull rear, an Atlas hydraulic crane and externally mounted

containers for additional engineering equipment. The vehicle can carry a mine-clearing plough, a rocket-propelled mine-clearing system, an aluminium track-way and a front-mounted dozer blade.

## SPECIFICATION:

**Chieftain AVLB**
**Crew:** 9.6
**Armament:** 1 x 7.62 mm machine-gun
**Ammunition:** 1,000 rounds
**Dimensions:** length (Chieftain Mk 5 hull) 7.52 m; height (Chieftain Mk 5 overall) 2.90 m; width (Chieftain Mk 5) 3.50 m; ground clearance (Chieftain Mk 5) 0.51 m
**Weight:** loaded (with No. 8 bridge) 53,300 kg
**Engine:** Leyland L60 2-stroke 6-cylinder multi-fuel; output 750 hp
**Performance:** range (Chieftain Mk 5) 400–500 km; maximum speed (Chieftain Mk 5) 48 km/h; speed cross-country 40 km/h
**Armour:** steel

# CV90/105 Light Tank/Recce Vehicle

*Troops disembark from a CV9030*

THE **STRIDSFORDON 90** (also known as **Combat Vehicle 90**) family of light armoured vehicles was developed for the Swedish Army in the mid-1980s following the successful testing of five prototypes. The vehicles are jointly manufactured by the Swedish companies Hägglunds Vehicle (originally Hägglunds and Söner) who build the chassis and Bofors, who build the turrets and fit them onto the chassis. Production of the first CV90s (the **CV9040**) started in 1991, with the first deliveries in 1993. The CV9040 is the standard tank in the CV90 series and is fitted with a two-man turret on which is mounted a 40 mm main gun, which has fully automated traverse and elevation with manual override if required. A prototype 25 mm gun turret was also built, the CV 9025 IFV, but has not been put into production. The Norwegian armed forces have ordered a 30 mm version, the **CV9030N**, and a 105 mm gun turret (CV90105 TML) and 120 mm gun (CV90120) or 120 mm mortar (CV9) turret are also being trialled.

The CV90 infantry fighting vehicle carries a crew of three, with the driver seated in the front of the hull, his entrance hatch being positioned towards the top left of the well-sloped glacis plate. The engine compartment, housing a Scania DS14 diesel engine, is situated to the right of the driver. The two-man turret housing the gunner and commander is in the centre of the hull, slightly to the left. To the rear of the hull is a troop compartment that can carry up to eight infantry seated on either side, facing inwards. Access is through a large door in the vertical hull rear, and roof hatches are also provided, but there are no firing ports

in the hull. The suspension consists of seven road wheels either side, the upper part being covered by an undulating shaped skirt.

The CV90 family includes a number of variants: the forward command vehicle, the forward observation vehicle, the armoured recovery vehicle; the TriAD 40 mm self-propelled anti-aircraft gun and the 30 mm-turret CV9030N. All are fitted with passive night vision equipment and an NBC system. A number of additional trial and concept vehicles have also been built: the CV90105 TML turret, the CV-90120 light tank, the CV9 mortar and the CV90 anti-tank concept. CV90 vehicles have been sold only to the Swedish and Norwegian armed forces.

## SPECIFICATION:

**Crew:** 3 + 8
**Armament:** 1 x 40 mm gun, 1 x 7.62 coaxial machine-gun, 6 x smoke grenade launchers
**Ammunition:** 238 rounds, 40 mm; 3,000 rounds, 7.62 mm
**Dimensions:** length 6.47 m; height (turret roof ) 2.50 m, (hull top) 1.73 m; width 3.00 m; ground clearance 0.45 m
**Weight:** loaded 22,800 kg; ground pressure 0.53 kg/cm$^2$
**Engine:** Scania DS14 diesel; output 550 hp
**Performance:** range 500 km; maximum speed 70 km/h
**Armour:** steel

# CVRT Scorpion Family Light Tank/Recce Vehicle

*Alvis Samaritan armoured ambulance*

I N THE EARLY 1960s THE BRITISH ARMY decided it needed to replace the 6 x 6 Saladin armoured car with a tracked armoured vehicle that had comparable armament but greater cross-country mobility. The **CVRT** (Combat Vehicle Reconnaissance [Tracked]) **Scorpion** family was developed to answer this need. The first prototype was built by Alvis of Coventry in 1969, and co-production started in Britain and Malines, Belgium, in 1971, with the first vehicles being delivered to the British and Belgian armies in 1972. The Scorpion was intended to fulfil a number of roles on the battlefield, and the basic design has been adapted to create a large family of armed fighting vehicles made up of the **FV101** Scorpion armed reconnaissance vehicle with the L23A1 76 mm gun (a lightweight development of the gun on the Saladin); the **Scorpion 90**, which is an upgraded FV101, the main gun being replaced by the heavier Belgian-built Cockerill 90 mm Mk III gun; the **FV102 Striker** anti-tank vehicle with five Swingfire anti-tank guided missile launchers; the **FV103 Spartan** armoured

personnel carrier, which has a two-man crew and can carry up to five infantry; the **FV104 Samaritan** ambulance; the **FV105 Sultan** command vehicle; the **FV106 Samson** recovery vehicle; the **FV107 Scimitar** reconnaissance vehicle with 30 mm gun, the Scorpion 90 armed reconnaissance vehicle with 90 mm gun; the prototype **Streaker** high-mobility load carrier; and the **Sabre**, which has a Vickers Defence Systems Fox light armoured car turret with 30 mm cannon and 7.62 mm coaxial machine-gun mounted on a Scorpion chassis. The **Stormer** APC is also based on Scorpion components.

In order to keep the weight down, allowing it to be mobile on the ground with a top speed of 80.5 km/h, and air-portable, the basic Scorpion hull and turret are of all-welded aluminium construction. The combination of the light weight of the vehicle and wide tracks gives the Scorpion a low ground pressure, enabling it to operate effectively over soft ground. The Scorpion can be made fully amphibious by erecting a collapsible flotation screen mounted on the

*Alvis Spartan APC of the British Army in Bosnia*

top of the hull (although British Army vehicles have removed the flotation screen). The vehicle is propelled through the water using its tracks at a maximum of 8 km/h. The main armament is a 76 mm gun firing HESH, HE and smoke projectiles, although some later versions have been fitted with a 90 mm gun which fires HEAT, HESH and HE, as well as smoke rounds. The 90 mm version carries fewer rounds (36) than the 40 rounds carried by the 76 mm Scorpion. Both versions also have a 7.62 mm coaxial machine-gun, with the option of an extra 7.62 mm anti-aircraft machine-gun mounted on the turret roof, and carry night vision equipment, as well as being fitted with an NBC system. Optional equipment

*Alvis Scimitar reconnaissance vehicle of the British Army in Bosnia*

*The Scorpion 90, armed with a 90 mm main armament, is in service with the Venezuelan Army*

includes a choice of fire-control systems, laser range-finders and air conditioning.

The Scorpion carries a crew of three. The driver sits at the front left of the vehicle, with the engine to his right and the transmission in front of him. The driver's hatch is positioned on the top left of the sloping glacis plate. The turret is mounted towards the rear of the hull and contains the commander on the left and the gunner on the right. The turret traverse through a full 360 degrees was manual on early models but later versions have been fitted with electrical drive. The original engine in the Scorpion was the Jaguar J60 4.2-litre six-cylinder sports car engine. This engine provided a high output and could be fitted within the confined space in the Scorpion, but concerns about the fire hazards of petrol have meant that many later Scorpions have been fitted with the Perkins T6-3544 turbo-charged 6-cylinder diesel engine, which produces 155 bhp. The fuel tank is located at the rear of the hull. The suspension has five large road wheels on either side plus a drive sprocket at the front and an idler at the back. It has no track return rollers.

Production ceased in the mid-1990s, and the 76 mm Scorpion is no longer in service in the British and Belgian armies, although others in the family are. However, Scorpions have been sold around the world (nearly 4,000 being produced in total) and are in service in many other countries: Botswana, Brunei, Chile, Indonesia, Iran, Ireland, Jordan, Kuwait, Malaysia, New Zealand, Nigeria, Oman, the Philippines, Spain, Tanzania, Thailand, Togo, United Arab Emirates and Venezuela. The Scorpion has seen action with the British Army, most notably in the war against Argentina in the Falkland Islands in 1982 and in the Gulf War as part of the coalition forces against Iraq in 1991, acquitting itself well in both these extremely contrasting terrains.

### SPECIFICATION:

**Scorpion CVRT**
**Crew:** 3
**Armament:** 1 x 76 mm gun, 1 x 7.62 mm coaxial machine-gun, 8 x smoke grenade dischargers
**Ammunition:** 40 rounds, 76 mm; 3,000 rounds, 7.62 mm
**Dimensions:** length 4.79 m; height 2.10 m; width 2.24 m; ground clearance 0.36 m
**Weight:** loaded 8,073 kg; ground pressure 0.36 kg/cm$^2$
**Engine:** Jaguar J60 4.2-litre 6-cylinder petrol; output 190 hp
**Performance:** range 644 km; maximum speed 80.5 km/h; speed cross-country 50 km/h
**Armour:** aluminium

# Dardo IFV

DEVELOPED UNDER THE NAME of **VCC-80 IV** by Consorzio Iveco OTO, Italy, production of the **Dardo** IFV by the same company to fulfil an order for 200 vehicles for the Italian Army started in 1998. The infantry fighting vehicle carries a crew of three. The driver is positioned at the front left of the all-aluminium armoured hull with a reinforcing steel layer. The engine compartment, housing an Iveco 8260 V-6 turbo-charged intercooled diesel developing 520 hp, is to the right of the driver. The driver's hatch is at the top left of the sloping glacis plate. The two-man turret is mounted on the centre of the hull. The commander is positioned on the left in the turret, with the gunner to his right. The commander's cupola is on the left of the turret roof with a periscopic sight in front of it. Mounted on the turret, which traverses through the full 360 degrees, is the stabilised 25 mm Oerlikon Contraves KBA cannon with power elevation, a 7.62 mm coaxial machine-gun to the left of the main gun and six smoke grenade launchers. Additional armament on an anti-tank version comprises two TOW (Tube-launched Optically-tracked Wire command-link guided) ATGW (Anti-Tank Guided Weapon) missile launchers. The Dardo is also fitted with a fire-control system with laser rangefinder and thermal image passive night vision equipment, and an NBC system. To the rear of the hull is situated the troop compartment, housing six infantry, five of whom can fire from the vehicle through two firing ports in each side of the hull and one in the rear ramp, each of which has a vision block above. Access to the troop compartment is via the large power-operated

*Dardo IFV armed with a 25 mm cannon and TOW ATGW launcher on each side of the turret*

ramp at the hull rear or a roof hatch in the roof above. The suspension has six road wheels on either side, with a drive sprocket at the front, an idler at the rear and three track-return rollers partly covered by a skirt.

The Dardo has been ordered to date only by the Italian Army. There is also a command post vehicle variant and an ambulance variant.

## SPECIFICATION:

**Crew:** 3 + 6
**Armament:** 1 x 25 mm gun, 1 x 7.62 mm coaxial machine-gun, 2 x TOW launchers, 6 x smoke grenade launchers
**Ammunition:** 200 rounds, 25 mm; 700 rounds 7.62 mm; 2 x TOW
**Dimensions:** length 6.71 m; height 2.64 m; width 3.00 m; ground clearance 0.40 m
**Weight:** empty 21,500 kg; loaded 23,000 kg; ground pressure 0.70 kg/cm$^2$
**Engine:** Iveco 8260 V-6 turbo-charged intercooled diesel; output 520 hp
**Performance:** range 500 km; maximum speed 70 km/h; speed cross-country 50 km/h
**Armour:** aluminium and steel

# ELBO Leonidas APC

*Leonidas APC of the Greek Army*

THE GREEK ARMY'S ELBO **LEONIDAS** armoured personnel carrier is essentially the Austrian Steyr 4K 7FA G127 APC produced under licence in Greece by ELBO, Hellenic Vehicle Industry SA. The Steyr 4K 7FA G127 was developed by Steyr-Daimler-Puch from the 4K 4FA series, the first prototype being completed in 1976 and the first production vehicles being delivered the following year. The first Greek **Leonidas 1** APC was completed in 1982, with production continuing until 1985. The vehicle has a crew of two. The driver is seated front left, with the engine compartment to his right, and the commander/gunner is seated in the cupola mounted on the hull behind the driver. The standard armament on the cupola is a 12.7 mm machine-gun, with four backward-firing smoke grenade dischargers mounted on the rear of the cupola. The Leonidas can also carry up to eight infantry in its troop compartment at the rear of the hull. Access to the troop compartment is via twin doors in the hull rear or roof hatches. Four pintle-mounted machine-guns can be fitted quickly to sockets around the top of the troop compartment to provide additional armament. The Leonidas uses the Steyr 7FA diesel engine, but has replaced the manual German ZF transmission in the Steyr 4K 7FA G127 with an automatic ZF transmission. Optional equipment for the Leonidas includes passive night vision equipment, an NBC system and a fire-detection and suppression system.

In 1987 the Greek Army placed a new order for further Leonidas APCs, and production of the **Leonidas 2** started. The vehicle was similar to its predecessor, with an additional fire-suppression system, commander's rotating periscope and improved smoke grenade dischargers. In 1992 the Greek Army also trialled three different turrets on a projected Leonidas

armoured infantry fighting vehicle (AIFV): a Spanish Santa Barbara TC-13 turret, a DAF/FMC enclosed weapon station and a Norwegian NFT T25 turret. Each turret was armed with a 25 mm gun and a 7.62 mm machine-gun. The Leonidas chassis has also been fitted with a Brazilian Engesa ET-90 turret and a French GIAT Industries TS-90 turret, both armed with a 90 mm gun. Also in 1998 the first prototype of an ELBO AIFV, called **Kentaurus**, was shown publicly. The company hopes this vehicle will eventually supersede the Leonidas, which is at present in service with the Greek Army and has also been sold to Cyprus.

## SPECIFICATION:

**Crew:** 2 + 8
**Armament:** 1 x 12.7 mm machine-gun, 4 x smoke grenade dischargers
**Ammunition:** 500 rounds, 12.7 mm
**Dimensions:** length 5.87 m; height (without armament) 1.61 m; width 2.50 m; ground clearance 0.42 m
**Weight:** loaded 14,800 kg; ground pressure 0.55 kg/cm$^2$
**Engine:** Steyr 7FA 6-cylinder liquid-cooled turbo-charged diesel; output 320 hp
**Performance:** range 520 km; maximum speed 70.6 km/h; speed cross-country 50 km/h
**Armour:** steel – 25 mm max.

# Engesa EE-3 Jararaca and EE-9 Cascavel Recce Vehicle

**P**OSTWAR, THE BRAZILIAN ARMY RELIED on imported AFVs until the 1970s, when it decided to use Brazilian-built vehicles. The Engesa company, São José dos Campos, developed a range of wheeled armoured vehicles starting with the EE-11 Urutu 6 x 6 armoured personnel carrier and the **EE-9 Cascavel** 6 x 6 armoured car, prototypes of both being delivered in 1970, and the first production vehicles being delivered in 1974. The **EE-3 Jararaca** 4 x 4 scout car was developed later in the decade. All the vehicles are named after local poisonous snakes.

The Cascavel, Jararaca and Urutu are manufactured using many components in common. The Cascavel has the same engine, transmission and suspension as the Urutu. The three-man crew comprises a driver front left, and a commander and gunner in the two-man turret, the commander on the left and the gunner on the right. The diesel engine and transmission are at the rear of the vehicle. The Cascavel has independent wishbone suspension on the front wheel on either side, and the back two wheels on either side are mounted close together on a boomerang walking beam suspension, which enables the vehicle to keep maximum contact with the ground over uneven terrain. Early Cascavels were fitted with a 37 mm main gun, but later a 90 mm gun was adopted. A 7.62 mm coaxial machine-gun is also fitted on the turret to the left of the main gun, and an additional 7.62 mm or 12.7 mm anti-aircraft machine-gun is mounted on a cupola on the turret, being aimed and fired from within the turret. Optional equipment includes a choice of either a Detroit Diesel engine generating 212 hp or a 190 hp Mercedes-Benz diesel engine. The range of Cascavels built runs from Mk I to Mk V, but there are no other variants.

The Jararaca 4 x 4 armoured car also has a crew of three. The driver is positioned at the front, with the machine-gunner behind to the right and the commander behind to the left. Access is through a large door on the right side of the hull. Equipment in the Jararaca and Cascavel includes passive night vision equipment, a central tyre-pressure-regulation

*Engesa EE-3 Jararaca 4 x 4 scout car*

*Engesa EE-9 Cascavel armoured car of the Zimbabwe Army*

system and tyres that can run when flat. The armament is mounted on the hull roof; options other than the standard 12.7 mm machine-gun include a Euromissile MILAN ATGW system, 7.62 mm machine-gun, 20 mm cannon, 60 mm mortar or a one-man turret on which is mounted a 20 mm cannon and a 7.62 mm machine-gun. There is a reconnaissance variant with an NBC monitoring system.

Production of the Engesa range of AFVs has ceased, and the company is no longer in existence. The Cascavel and the Jararaca are still in service in the Brazilian Army and have also been widely sold for export, the Jararaca being in service in Cyprus, Ecuador, Gabon and Uruguay, the Cascavel being in service in, amongst others, Bolivia, Burkina Faso, Chad, Chile, Colombia, Cyprus, Ecuador, Gabon, Ghana, Iran, Iraq, Libya, Nigeria, Paraguay, Surinam, Togo, Tunisia, Uruguay and Zimbabwe.

## SPECIFICATION:

**Cascavel**
**Crew:** 3
**Armament:** 1 x 90 mm gun, 1 x 7.62 mm coaxial machine-gun, 1 x 7.62 mm or 12.7 mm AA machine-gun, 6 x smoke grenade launchers
**Ammunition:** 44 rounds, 90 mm; 2,200 rounds, 7.62 mm
**Dimensions:** length 5.20 m; height (top of gun mounted) 2.28 m, (hull top) 1.56 m; width 2.64 m; ground clearance 0.34 m
**Weight:** empty 10,900 kg; loaded 13,400 kg
**Engine:** Detroit Diesel 6V-53N 6-cylinder water-cooled diesel; output 212 hp
**Performance:** range 880 km; maximum speed 100 km/h; speed cross-country 80 km/h
**Armour:** steel

**Jararaca**
**Crew:** 3
**Armament:** 1 x 12.7 mm machine-gun
**Ammunition:** 1,000 rounds, 12.7 mm
**Dimensions:** length 4.16 m; height (top of gun mounted) 2.30 m, (hull top) 1.56 m; width 2.24 m; ground clearance 0.34 m
**Weight:** loaded 5,800 kg
**Engine:** Mercedes-Benz OM 314A turbo-charged 4-cylinder water-cooled diesel; output 120 hp
**Performance:** range 700 km; maximum speed 100 km/h; speed cross-country 80 km/h
**Armour:** steel

# Fennek Multi-Purpose Carrier Recce Vehicle

*Fennek reconnaissance vehicle of the German Army with sensor pod extended*

THE **FENNEK MULTI-PURPOSE CARRIER** (MPC) has been developed as a joint venture for the German and Dutch armies by the private company SP Aerospace and Vehicle Systems, Geldrop, Netherlands. The first of four protoypes was built in 1992, two being trialled by the Dutch Army and two by the German Army, with both armies placing orders. Construction of the vehicle is undertaken by SP Aerospace and Vehicle Systems, with Krauss-Maffei Wegmann of Germany being responsible for the systems integration.

The MPC has a crew of three within the aluminium hull. The driver is seated at the front behind a large bullet-proof windscreen, which is set back behind the sloping nose at the front of the vehicle, and there are bullet-proof windows either side of the driver which slope back towards the rear. The other two crew members, usually a commander and a radio operator, are seated in the middle of the vehicle. Access is via a large forward-opening door on each side of the hull or roof hatches in the forward part of the flat hull roof. The engine compartment, housing a 6-cylinder turbo-charged diesel engine developing 240 hp and giving the vehicle a high maximum speed of 115 km/h, is at the rear of the hull, where the hull slopes down at the back. The suspension has two large road wheels on either side. The armament is

mounted on the hull, the standard weapon being a 7.62 mm machine-gun carrying 1,000 rounds, although other machine-guns, ATGWs and smoke grenade launchers can be fitted. Night vision and NBC equipment can also be fitted.

The Fennek is intended to be used in a variety of roles, including battlefield surveillance and command and control. Amphibious equipment can also be fitted. A reconnaissance version, the **LBV**, is also being developed for the Dutch and German armies.

---

## SPECIFICATION:

**Crew:** 3
**Armament:** 1 x 7.62 mm machine-gun
**Ammunition:** 1,000 rounds, 7.62 mm
**Dimensions:** length 5.71 m; height 1.79 m; width 2.49 m
**Weight:** empty 7,900 kg; loaded 9,600 kg
**Engine:** 6-cylinder turbo-charged intercooled diesel; output 240 hp
**Performance:** range 800 km; maximum speed 115 km/h; speed cross-country 50 km/h
**Armour:** aluminium

# Fuchs APC/AIFV

*The Fuchs NBC reconnaissance vehicle was used by the British Army during the Gulf War of 1991*

SUPPLIED BY HENSCHEL WEHRTECHNIK, Kassel, Germany, for the German Army from 1979, the **Transportpanzer 1** 6 x 6 armoured personnel carrier, known as **Fuchs**, has since been sold to a number of countries worldwide. The original vehicle was developed from a number of prototypes of amphibious load carriers, but since the late 1980s Henschel has produced an NBC reconnaissance version which has also been sold to the US Army, where it is known as the **M93**, and was used in the Gulf War in 1991.

The two-man crew, comprising a driver and commander are positioned at the front of the vehicle, with the engine compartment behind them. Above the glacis plate is a large one-piece window covered by a hinged armoured shutter. Access to the crew compartment is via two large outward-opening doors either side of the window and two hatches at the front of the roof. A small passageway leads into the troop compartment, extending to the rear of the vehicle, which can carry up to ten infantry. Access to the troop compartment is via twin doors at the rear of the steel hull. The standard armament is a 7.62 mm machine-gun mounted on the front of the hull roof, with a bank of six forward-firing smoke grenade launchers on the left side of the hull. The suspension has three large road wheels on either side with an axle ground clearance of 0.41 m. The Fuchs is fully amphibious, being driven through the water by two propellers mounted at the back underneath the hull, and there is a retractable trim vane on the glacis plate.

The Fuchs Transportpanzer 1 is still in production and is in service in Germany, Israel, the Netherlands,

Saudi Arabia, Turkey, the UK, the USA and Venezuela. The upgraded version is the **Fuchs KRK** with improved armour and increased payload. Standard equipment includes an NBC system, power-assisted steering on the front two axles and an engine compartment fire-extinguisher system. A wide range of variants are available, including a command and communications vehicle, the RASIT radar carrier, an engineer/ demolitions vehicle, a supply carrier, an electronic warfare vehicle, an ambulance, an 81 mm or 120 mm mortar vehicle, a cargo carrier, a recovery or maintenance vehicle and an infantry fighting vehicle with firing ports in the hull sides.

## SPECIFICATION:

**Crew:** 2 + 10
**Armament:** 1 x 7.62 mm machine-gun, 6 x smoke grenade launchers
**Ammunition:** 1,000 rounds, 7.62 mm
**Dimensions:** length 6.30 m; height (hull top) 2.30 m; ground clearance (hull) 0.51 mm, (axle) 0.41 m
**Weight:** empty 14,400 kg; loaded 19,000 kg
**Engine:** Mercedes-Benz Model OM 402A V-8 liquid-cooled diesel; output 320 hp
**Performance:** range 800 km; maximum speed 105 km/h; speed cross-country 80 km/h
**Armour:** steel

# Hägglunds BV206S APC/AIFV

THE **BV206S** WAS DEVELOPED BY Hägglunds Vehicle (now owned by Alvis plc, UK) in conjunction with the Swedish Army. The first prototypes were completed in 1989 and the first production vehicles delivered to the Swedish Army later the same year.

The Hägglunds BV206S is a unique all-terrain armoured personnel carrier on the modern battlefield. The vehicle consists of two separate all-welded steel bodies linked together by a steering unit which uses two hydraulic cylinders servo-controlled by a conventional steering wheel. Both units are mounted on wide rubber-band-type tracks and are intended to protect the occupants from shell splinters and small-arms fire up to 7.62 mm at point-blank range. The windows provide the same level of armour protection as the steel hull. The front unit carries the crew of two, comprising a driver and commander, with the engine compartment housing the Steyr diesel engine, which generates 186 hp and gives the vehicle a top road speed of 50 km/h, in the sloping bonnet in the front of the vehicle. There are two additional seats at the back of the front unit for two passengers. The front unit has a two-part windscreen at the front of the body. Access for the crew is via a door on each side of the unit, and there are a further two smaller windows on either side, one above each door and one set further back. The rear unit is, in effect, the troop compartment, carrying up to eight infantry. Access is via a large door at the back of the unit, which has two windows. The standard armament is a 12.7 mm machine-gun mounted on the roof of the front unit, but alternatively a 7.62 mm machine-gun or 40 mm grenade launcher could be mounted. A 140 mm twin

*The Hägglunds BV206S APC is used by France, Germany, Sweden and the Royal Marines*

recoilless rifle system has also been trialled. The BV206S is fully amphibious, propelling itself through the water by its tracks, and is also air-portable, being able to be carried by helicopter or fixed-wing aircraft. Optional equipment includes an NBC system, night vision equipment and a recovery winch. The vehicle can also be adapted into an ambulance, command post vehicle, recovery vehicle or weapons carrier (a 120 mm mortar carrier version is being developed for the German Army). It is still in production with Hägglunds Vehicle OB and is in service with the Swedish and French armies, as well as being approved for service by the German Army.

## SPECIFICATION:

**Crew:** 4 + 8
**Armament:** 1 x 12.7 mm machine-gun
**Dimensions:** length 6.88 m; height (unit roof top) 1.90 m; width 2.00 m; ground clearance 0.35 m
**Weight:** empty 5,300 kg; loaded 7,000 kg
**Engine:** Steyr M16 6-cylinder in-line diesel; output 186 hp
**Performance:** range 370 km; maximum speed 50 km/h; speed cross-country 40 km/h
**Armour:** steel

# GERMANY
# Jagdpanzer Jaguar Tank Destroyer

THE **JAGDPANZER JAGUAR 1** self-propelled ATGW vehicle is based on a German anti-tank missile vehicle, the Jagdpanzer Rakete, which was built in the mid-1960s. Construction of the Jagdpanzer Rakete was undertaken by two companies, Hanomag and Henschel, and the vehicles used the same chassis as an earlier self-propelled anti-tank gun, the 90 mm Jagdpanzer Kanone (JPZ 4-5) built by the two companies. The Jagdpanzer Jaguar 1, the latest in a long line of specialised tank-hunter vehicles used by the German Army since World War II, was developed by rebuilding original Raketes between 1978 and 1983. Thyssen Henschel (now Henschel Wehrtechnik) undertook the conversion work, and the original SS-11 ATGW was replaced by the more advanced K3S HOT ATGW system, supplied by Euromissile. The missile launcher can be retracted, but when in action is situated on the left side of the fighting compartment, being retracted under the armour for reloading. The missile is packed in the tube clipped to the launcher and has a maximum range of 4,000 m. Thyssen Henschel also added appliqué armour to the glacis plate and fighting compartment sides to provide better protection against HEAT missiles. In addition the Jagdpanzer Jaguar 1 carries a 7.62 mm MG3 bow machine-gun on the right side of the front of hull. A second 7.62 mm anti-aircraft machine-gun can be mounted on the commander's cupola, and eight forward-firing smoke grenade dischargers are mounted on the rear of the hull. The fighting compartment containing the four-man crew is located in the front of the turretless steel hull. The engine compartment housing the Daimler-Benz MB 837 8-cylinder water-cooled diesel (which was also used in the Jagdpanzer Rakete) is situated at the rear of the vehicle. The suspension has five road wheels on either side, with the idler at the front and the drive sprocket at the rear. The return rollers are covered by armoured skirts with a wavy line at the bottom.

*A Jaguar 1 of Panzergrenadierlehrbatallion 92 (VS-Books Carl Schulze)*

The **Jaguar 2** is a variant on the earlier Jagdpanzer Kanone JPZ 4-5 design, with the 90 mm gun removed and appliqué armour and a roof-mounted TOW ATGW launcher added. The conversion was carried out by Henschel Wehrtechnik between 1983 and 1985. A prototype with a HOT compact turret and four HOT ATGWs in ready-to-launch position has also been built. Production of the Jagdpanzer Jaguar 1 is now complete, and the SP tank destroyer is in service with the German and Austrian armies.

*Jagdpanzer Jaguar 1 with HOT missile in firing position*

## SPECIFICATION:

**Crew:** 4
**Armament:** 1 x HOT ATGW launcher, 1 x 7.62 mm machine-gun, 1 x 7.62 mm AA machine-gun, 8 x smoke grenade dischargers
**Ammunition:** 20 rounds, HOT ATGW; 3,200 rounds, 7.62 mm
**Dimensions:** length 6.61 m; height (including missile launcher) 2.54 m, (hull top) 1.98 m; width 3.12 m; ground clearance (front) 0.45 m, (rear) 0.44 m
**Weight:** loaded 25,500 kg; ground pressure 0.70 kg/cm$^2$
**Engine:** Daimler-Benz MB 837 8-cylinder water-cooled diesel; output 500 hp
**Performance:** range 400 km; maximum speed 70 km/h; speed cross-country 50 km/h
**Armour:** steel – 50 mm

# LAV-150 APC/AIFV

*LAV-150/20 with 20 mm gun turret*

THE HIGHLY VERSATILE CADILLAC GAGE range of light-armoured vehicles has been in US Army service since the first production Commando LAV-100s (US Army designation M706) were completed in 1964. A larger version with a bigger engine, the LAV-200, was also built at the time for sale to Singapore. Cadillac Gage (later Textron Marine & Land Systems, New Orleans) replaced the LAV-100 and LAV-200 in production in 1971 with the **LAV-150**. The new vehicle, with improved armour, used a V-8 diesel engine as a replacement for the petrol engine used in the earlier models. In 1985 the LAV-150 was upgraded to the heavier and longer **LAV-150S**. The LAV-150, as the previous versions, operates with a three-man crew, with the commander and gunner at the front of the welded steel hull. The troop compartment, which can carry two or three infantry, is at the rear of the hull and has three firing ports with vision blocks in the upper half of the doors. The engine compartment is also at the rear, to the left. Access is via the three doors, one on each side and one in the rear. The vehicle is fully amphibious, being propelled through the water by its large road wheels (which have run-flat capacity). A winch is also mounted on the front of the hull. The utility hull of the LAV-150 can be fitted with a wide range of armament, both turret and hull-roof mounted, including a one- or two-man turret. The range of options includes a 20 mm cannon and 7.62 mm coaxial machine-gun plus 7.62 mm anti-aircraft machine-gun; two-man turret with 90 mm gun and two 7.62 mm machine-guns; 81 mm mortar, TOW ATGW, two 7.62 mm machine-guns; one 7.62 mm and one 12.7 mm machine-gun; 25 mm cannon and 7.62 mm machine-gun; 40 mm grenade launcher and 12.7 mm machine-gun, or 20 mm cannon.

In addition to the wide range of armament carried by the LAV-150, a number of variants have been built, including the **LAV-300** 6 x 6 version and the **ASV 150** (armoured security vehicle), plus ambulances, recovery vehicles and command vehicles. Many countries have bought the LAV-150, including Botswana, Cameroon, Chad, Dominican Republic, Gabon, Guatemala, Haiti, Indonesia, Jamaica, Kuwait, Malaysia, Mexico, the Philippines, Saudi Arabia, Singapore, Sudan, Taiwan, Thailand, Turkey and Venezuela. Over the years the LAV has seen action in many theatres of war, the LAV-100 being particularly widely used in the conflict in Vietnam in the 1960s and 1970s.

## SPECIFICATION:

**Crew:** 3 + 2
**Armament:** (many variants) 1 x 20 mm, 1 x 7.62 mm coaxial machine-gun, 1 x 7.62 mm AA machine-gun, 12 x smoke grenade launchers
**Ammunition:** 400 rounds, 20 mm; 3,200 rounds, 7.62 mm
**Dimensions:** length 5.69 m; height (turret roof) 2.54 m, (hull roof) 1.98 m; width 2.26 m; ground clearance (axle) 0.38 m, (hull) 0.65 m
**Weight:** loaded 9,888 kg
**Engine:** V-504 V-8 diesel; output 202 hp
**Performance:** range 643 km; maximum speed 88.5 km/h; speed cross-country 50 km/h
**Armour:** steel

# LAV-25 Light Tank/Recce Vehicle

*LAV-25 (Reconnaissance) with dismounted sensor suite of battlefield surveillance radar deployed*

IN THE LATE 1970S/EARLY 1980s the US Marine Corps and the US Army decided they needed a new LAV (light armoured vehicle) which would be fully amphibious, could be easily transported by air and could be adapted without difficulty for a wide range of roles anywhere in the world. In 1981 testing started of prototype vehicles from three rival companies. Alvis, UK, submitted the Scorpion 90 and the Stormer APC with a 25 mm cannon turret; Cadillac Gage, USA, submitted the 4 x 4 V-150 Commando and the 6 x 6 V-300 Commando, and General Motors of Canada submitted an 8 x 8 version of the Swiss MOWAG Piranha built under licence in Canada as the Cougar. In 1982 the contract was awarded to Diesel Division, General Motors of Canada, for the MOWAG Piranha, and although subsequently the US Army pulled out of the agreement, the US Marine Corps ordered six basic versions of what became the **LAV-25**, built in London, Ontario. The first production vehicles were delivered in 1983, with the final vehicles of the order being delivered in 1987. However, production of the vehicles is still continuing as the LAV-25's advantages of adaptability, its mobility compared to tracked vehicles, with a top speed of 100 km/h, allowing it to be quickly deployed, and its relative cheapness to build and operate, attract buyers abroad as well as in the US armed forces.

The basic LAV-25 carries a crew of three. The driver is seated at the front left of the vehicle, with the engine compartment housing the 275 hp 6-cylinder Detroit Diesel engine to the right. The two-man power-operated tower is mounted behind the driver, containing the commander and the gunner. Turret traverse is through a full 360 degrees. At the rear of the vehicle is a troop compartment which can hold six Marines seated facing outwards, three on each side, with a firing port and vision block for each Marine. Access to the troop compartment is via two doors in the hull rear. The standard armament on the two-man turret, which is the same as that fitted to the US Army's M2 Bradley infantry fighting vehicle, consists of a 25 mm M242 chain gun plus a coaxial M240 7.62 mm machine-gun. Additional armament comprises either another 7.62 mm or 12.7 mm anti-aircraft machine-gun mounted on the turret roof, although the adaptability of the LAV enables a wide range of armament to be fitted, and variants for export have been built with a 120 mm armoured mortar system, 90 mm gun and HOT ATGW. The LAV-25 is fully amphibious, being driven through the water up to a maximum speed of 10.4 km/h by two propellers mounted at the rear of the hull. Before entering the water a trim vane is raised and the bilge pumps switched on. Standard additional equipment on the LAV-25 includes power-assisted steering for the front four wheels and a full range of passive night vision equipment for all the crew.

The six original versions of the LAV originally delivered to the USMC are a two-man logistics vehicle with a crane on a raised roof; an 81 mm

mortar carrier with the armament mounted at the rear; the standard LAV-25 with 25 mm cannon; an anti-tank LAV with a three-man crew and Hughes Improved TOW ATGW, two of which are in the ready-to-launch position; a maintenance and recovery vehicle which has a five-man crew; and a command and control vehicle with a raised hull similar to that of the logistics vehicle. Since then other variants have been produced, including a Mobile Electronic Warfare Support system vehicle (MEWS) with raised roof, an armoured personnel carrier with a 7.62 mm machine-gun, which carries a crew of two plus nine troops, called the **Bison**, an armoured personnel carrier variant with LAV 25 mm turret known as the **Kodiak**, and a reconnaissance version for the Canadian Army with 25 mm turret plus mast sensors known as the **Coyote**. A number of prototypes have also been developed, including an anti-aircraft LAV fitted with a turret armed with 25 mm cannon and Stinger surface-to-air missiles, and an assault gun vehicle armed with a 105 mm gun.

The LAV-25 is still in production and is in service in Australia, Canada, Saudi Arabia and with the US Army and Marine Corps. The US Air Force has also express-ed an interest in a mobile armoured reconnaissance vehicle/stand-off munition device (MARV/SMUD) which can be used on airfields after an enemy attack for explosive ordnance disposal (EOD).

*The LAV-25 has been used in combat by the US Marine Corps during the conflict in Afghanistan*

## SPECIFICATION:

**Crew:** 3 + 6
**Armament:** 1 x 25 mm gun, 1 x 7.62 mm coaxial machine-gun, 1 x 7.62 mm AA machine-gun, 8 smoke grenade dischargers
**Ammunition:** 630 rounds, 25 mm; 1,620 rounds, 7.62 mm
**Dimensions:** length 6.39 m; height 2.69 m; width 2,50 m; ground clearance 0.50 m
**Weight:** empty 10,932 kg; loaded 12,882 kg
**Engine:** General Motors Detroit Diesel 6V-53T 6-cylinder diesel; output 275 hp
**Performance:** range 668 km; maximum speed 100 km/h; speed cross-country 80 km/h
**Armour:** steel – 10 mm

# Leclerc Engineer ARV and Engineer Vehicle

**The Leclerc Poseur de Travures du Génie**

IN 1997 GIAT INDUSTRIES, FRANCE, started promoting a range of variants of its Leclerc MBT first produced in 1991. The variants were designated **E-Force**, or **Engineer-Force**, and comprised the **Leclerc ARV** (armoured recovery vehicle, also known as DNG – *Dépanneur Nouvelle Génération*), the K2D mine-clearing kit, the **EPG armoured engineer vehicle** (*Engin Principal du Génie*) and the **PTG** (*Poseur de Travures du Génie*) armoured-vehicle-launched bridge. The only variant to enter production by 2000 was the ARV, the first prototype being completed in 1994. The Leclerc ARV has been ordered by the United Arab Emirates, which has received its first production vehicles, and the French Army. The Leclerc MBT is also in service only in France and the United Arab Emirates, and the new ARV is required to recover, tow or repair a disabled tank, as the current French AMX-30D ARV cannot recover the heavier Leclerc. The Leclerc ARV has a longer chassis than the MBT, with seven road wheels on each side rather than the MBT's six, and a new superstructure, but it uses the same power-pack, SAMM hydropneumatic suspension and track-tensioning systems. The recovery equipment is

**The Leclerc Engin Principal du Génie**

*A Dépanneur Nouvelle Génération Leclerc ARV of the United Arab Emirates Army negotiates the rolling sand dunes of the Arabian desert. (Giat Industries Leclerc)*

supplied by MaK of Germany and comprises a hydraulic crane which can lift a maximum of 30 tonnes, a main winch with a maximum pull of 35 tonnes and an auxiliary winch. A hydraulically operated dozer blade is mounted at the front of the ARV to stabilise the vehicle when the crane or winch is used, or to clear obstacles. The K2D mine-clearing kit can also be fitted to the ARV, which comprises a Pearson Engineering Full Width Mineplough fitted to the front of the vehicle and includes a DEMETER electromagnetic signature duplicator designed to trigger magnetic mines ahead of the vehicle, a Pearson Engineering Pathfinder dual minefield marking system, and a Pronit rocket-propelled mine-clearing system either side of the rear of the hull. A GIAT Industries Minotaur mine-scattering system can also be installed.

The projected Leclerc EPG armoured engineer vehicle has the same hydraulic crane and winches as the ARV but can also be fitted with additional specialised engineering equipment, e.g. a bucket, augur, grapple, hammer or hook, and can carry fascines. A remote-controlled cupola with a 142 mm demolition gun and a 12.7 mm machine-gun is mounted on the hull roof. Optional equipment includes ERA armour, remote-control capability, thermal imaging and a FINDERS navigation system.

The projected PTG armoured-vehicle-launched bridge is also based on the Leclerc MBT, with the turret replaced by Vickers' Universal Bridge Launching Equipment, which can lay a No. 10 bridge spanning 26 m or a No. 12 bridge spanning 13.5 m.

# Leclerc Main Battle Tank

*Leclerc Main Battle Tank (Tim Ripley)*

**D**URING THE 1970s THE FRENCH and West German armies started collaborating on a project to build a new main battle tank to replace the French AMX-30 B2 and the German Leopard 1 MBT. The joint venture collapsed in 1982, but the French Army continued to develop the design of what they called at the time the AMX-48, building a number of test rigs, and produced their own first prototype in 1989 of what was to be called the **Leclerc** (after a French World War II general). The tank entered production in 1990 and by 1992 the first Leclercs were being delivered to the French Army. In the following year the United Arab Emirates also ordered the Leclerc. The tank is built by GIAT Industries at two sites, the turret at GIAT Tarbes and the chassis at GIAT Roanne, where the final assembly also takes place.

Although similar in size and armament to its main rival Western MBTs – the German Leopard 2, the British Challenger 2 and the US Abrams M1A1 – the Leclerc has only a three-man crew rather than the conventional four, with the loader being replaced by an automatic loader. The driver is seated towards the front left of the hull, although well behind the sloping glacis plate, and has a drum of some of the 120 mm ammunition stowed to his right. The other crew members are positioned in the power-operated two-man turret set in the centre of the hull. The commander is seated to the left of the main gun and the gunner on the right, again differing from the conventional layout, which has the commander on the right and the gunner on the left. Both hull and

turret are constructed of welded steel with added modular composite armour, which gives high resistance to kinetic and chemical attack and can be easily upgraded. The Leclerc's long, low turret (markedly different from the upright turret seen on the prototype) is electrically powered (with emergency manual controls) and carries the main GIAT 120-26 120 mm smooth-bore gun. The gun's chamber has the same dimensions as those in US and German guns, ensuring commonality of ammunition, although the muzzle is longer, giving a high muzzle velocity to the missile fired. The gun also has a thermal sleeve and expels the gases using compressed air. The automatic loader, manufactured by Creusot-Loire, holds 22 rounds of ready-to-use ammunition and is mounted in the long turret bustle, separated from the crew in the rest of the turret by an armoured bulkhead with blow-out panels in the roof which divert the blast in the event of an explosion, to further protect the crew. The commander or gunner selects one of a choice of five different types of ammunition, basically divided between HEAT and APFSDS rounds, which the automatic loader loads at a rate of up to 12 rounds a minute. Additional armament consists of a remote-controlled GIAT M693 (F2) 12.7 mm coaxial machine-gun (again differing from the more conventional 7.62 mm), and an NFI

*Leclerc Main Battle Tank (Tim Ripley)*

7.62 mm anti-aircraft machine-gun mounted on the turret roof. There are also 18 smoke grenade launchers on the turret roof. The turret has a distinctive profile, having several periscopes, including the commander's large periscope on the left side of the turret.

The Leclerc is powered by a SACM V8X 8-cylinder diesel engine which generates 1,500 hp, giving the tank a high power-to-weight ratio. (This allows the armour to be upgraded in the future without a serious loss of mobility.) The engine is housed in a slightly raised compartment at the rear of the hull. A Turbomeca TM-7038 gas turbine is also installed to provide power when the tank is stationary, enabling the main engine to be shut down. Additional long-range fuel tanks can be fitted at the rear of the hull to increase the tank's range from its basic 550 km. The hydropneumatic suspension has six tracked road wheels either side, an idler at the front, a drive sprocket at the rear and track return rollers. The top half of the suspension is covered by an armoured skirt.

Additional equipment fitted to the Leclerc includes an NBC system, a fire-detection and suppression system, a computerised battle management system comprising a COTAC fire-control system, including optical sights, low-light TV sight, sensors, a laser rangefinder and passive night vision equipment.

The Leclerc MBT is still in production. The **Leclerc Mk 2** with improved software and climate control systems entered production in 1998, as did the **Leclerc Armoured Recovery Vehicle**. Both have been sold to the French and United Arab Emirates' armies. Two other variants have been projected: the PTG armoured-vehicle-launched bridge and the EPG armoured engineer vehicle. A K2D mine-clearing kit can also be fitted to the Leclerc ARV or Leclerc EPG.

---

## SPECIFICATION:

**Crew:** 3

**Armament:** 1 x 120 mm gun, 1 x 12.7 mm coaxial machine-gun, 1 x 7.62 mm AA machine-gun, 18 x smoke grenade launchers

**Ammunition:** 40 rounds, 120 mm; 578 rounds, 20 mm; 2,170 rounds, 7.62 mm

**Dimensions:** length (gun forwards) 9.87 m, (hull) 6.88 m; height 2.53 m; width 3.71 m; ground clearance 0.50 m

**Weight:** loaded 54,500 kg; ground pressure 0.9 kg/cm²

**Engine:** SACM V8X 8-cylinder liquid-cooled; output 1,500 hp

**Performance:** range 550 km; maximum speed 71 km/h; speed cross-country 50 km/h

**Armour:** steel/composite/laminate

# Leopard 1 Flakpanzer SP Artillery

*Flakpanzer Gepard or Cheetah*

WHEN WEST GERMANY JOINED NATO in 1955 the country needed to develop a new German main battle tank, the first since World War II, as part of the rebuilding of the German armed forces. Development of the **Leopard 1**, which would become one of the most successful postwar designs of tank, started in the late 1950s, at first jointly with France and Italy, but after these two countries pulled out of the project the Germans continued the development alone, with the first production Leopard 1s being delivered in 1965. At the same time the Germans, in the front line during the Cold War and remembering the devastation wrought by Allied fighter-bombers on panzer formations in World War II, decided that anti-aircraft protection of their armour was vital and that a gun-armed anti-aircraft tank was best able to fulfil this role. Using the Leopard as its base, the **Flakpanzer Gepard** anti-aircraft self-propelled gun was developed. The first Gepards were delivered in 1974, with production continuing until 1976, the vehicle being manufactured by Krauss-Maffei Wegmann, Munich, who also built the Leopard MBT. As well as being in service with the German Army, it has been sold to the Netherlands (where it is known as the **CA1 Caesar**) and Belgium.

Several prototype anti-aircraft systems were trialled before the twin 35 mm Oerlikon cannon were adopted. Early attempts to fit a 30 mm twin gun onto an APC chassis failed because the APC was too small to fit the complex fire-control system, but the larger chassis allowed both the larger twin 35 mm guns and the surveillance and fire-control radars to be fitted on the one vehicle to produce the Gepard. The Gepard's weapon system, which is fitted into the turret, comprises a search radar, a tracking radar and a computerised fire-control system, and the twin 35 mm guns are fitted onto trunnions towards the rear of the turret, which gives maximum elevation without compromising the armour protection, and also avoids problems of spent cartridges and fumes. The 35 mm Oerlikon cannon are intended to combat ground attack aircraft and tank-hunting helicopters, and can fire either APHE (Armour-Piercing High Explosive) or HEI (High Explosive Incendiary) ammunition at a maximum rate of 550 rounds per minute at a range of 3,500 m. The Gepard has a crew of three, comprising a driver, commander and a gunner, and the tank is powered by the same MTU diesel engine as the Leopard MBT. A separate diesel engine is housed in the hull to provide back-up power because of the high requirements for electrical power of the radar and tracking system.

## SPECIFICATION:

**Crew:** 3
**Armament:** 2 x 35 mm guns
**Ammunition:** 700 rounds, 35 mm
**Dimensions:** length (hull) 7.09 m; height 3.01 m; width 3.25 m; ground clearance 0.44 m
**Weight:** loaded 45,500 kg; ground pressure 0.95 kg/cm$^2$
**Engine:** MTU MB838 Ca-M500 10-cylinder water-cooled diesel; output 830 hp
**Performance:** range 550 km; maximum speed 65 km/h; speed cross-country 50 km/h
**Armour:** steel – 70 mm front, 35 mm sides, 25 mm rear

# GERMANY
# Leopard 1 Bridgelayer AVLB

THE **LEOPARD 1** MAIN BATTLE TANK was developed by West Germany in the 1950s, initially in conjunction with France and Italy. Although the other two countries pulled out, Germany went ahead with the design and the first Leopard 1 was delivered to the German Army in 1965. Since then it has become one of the most successful postwar MBT designs with its combination of firepower and mobility, and has been sold throughout the world, still being in service in many countries. A number of variants were also built over the years, including many specialised tanks. The **Leopard AVLB** (Armoured Vehicle-Launched Bridge) was manufactured by Atlas-MaK Maschinenbau, Kiel, between 1973 and 1975. The company did not build the main Leopard 1 MBT but did produce the ARV and AEV variants. Produced initially for the German Army, the armoured bridge-layer (**Bruckenlegepanzer**), nicknamed **Biber** (Beaver) uses the basic Leopard 1 chassis, without the turret.

Two prototypes were built in order to compare methods of horizontal bridgelaying. The first used an extensible telescopic system, on which the bridge was rolled out. The telescope was then retracted once the bridge was in place. The second design, developed by Klockner-Humboldt-Deutz, was the one chosen, and is unique on the battlefield. Unlike conventional bridgelayers which use a fold-out scissors or up-and-over bridge, the Biber carries its bridge in two symmetrical halves, using the weight of the tank as a cantilever to counterbalance the bridge. The Biber braces itself by pushing out a dozer blade at the front end of the hull into the ground. It then slides forward the lower half of the bridge, which forms the bridge's front end, the upper half then drops down and the two bridge halves lock together. The bridge is then pushed forward away from the chassis on to a cantilevered boom, which is lowered across the gap. Although more complicated to design

*Bruckenlegepanzer Biber or Beaver*

and operate, this system has the benefit of being less visible from a distance, providing a much lower target to the enemy, and potentially keeping the advantage of surprise in an advance. The bridge is made of light metal alloy, can span up to 20 m and carries vehicles of up to 50 tonnes. After use the Biber can cross the bridge and take it up again, carrying the two symmetrical halves of the bridge on top of its chassis, being connected by web plates.

The AVLB is in service with the German Army and has also been sold to Australia, Canada, the Netherlands and Norway. A new AVLB based on the Leopard 2 chassis is also projected for sale to the German and Dutch armies. The new vehicle, with a modular bridge system, will be built by MAN.

## SPECIFICATION:

**Crew:** 4
**Armament:** None
**Ammunition:** None
**Dimensions:** length 10.2 m (11.4 m with bridge); height 2.56 m (3.5 m with bridge); width 3.25 m (4.00 m with bridge); ground clearance 0.44 m
**Weight:** empty 35,000 kg (45,000 kg with bridge); ground pressure 0.96 kg/cm$^2$
**Engine:** MTU MB838 Ca-M500 10-cylinder water-cooled diesel; output 830 hp
**Performance:** range 800 km; maximum speed 62 km/h; speed cross-country 50 km/h
**Armour:** steel – 70 mm front, 35 mm sides, 25 mm back

# Leopard 2A6 MBT

*Leopard 2 MBT Strv-122 of the Swedish Army*

*Leopard 2 driver training tank*

THE GERMAN **LEOPARD MBT** HAS A LONG history. The Leopard 1, which was developed in the 1950s, was one of the most successful postwar tank designs, and is still in service in a number of countries worldwide. By the 1960s the Germans were looking ahead to develop a new MBT which would eventually replace the Leopard 1. As with the Leopard 1, the initial development of the new MBT was a collaborative venture, this time with the Americans, to build a standardised tank which could be used by a number of countries in NATO. A prototype, MTB70, was built, but the project was abandoned in 1970. The Germans, however, had already started on their own MBT project, called first **Kampfpanzer 2**, then **Keiler** (wild boar) and finally **Leopard 2**, and work continued on this, with several prototypes being completed by Krauss-Maffei (later Krauss-Maffei Wegmann) between 1972 and 1974. The specification was for an MBT which had improved firepower and protection compared with the Leopard 1, but with comparable mobility. It was also important that many components were compatible with the Leopard 1 so that the earlier tanks could be easily upgraded. Following extensive testing of the prototypes in Germany, Canada and the USA, the US Army, which was still looking for its own new MBT, decided to test two specially built prototype Leopard 2s, known as the **Leopard 2AV** (Austere Version) against a prototype US-designed XM1. After the tests the US Army decided not to recommend the Leopard, although it was agreed that, where possible, components would be harmonised in the new US and German tanks. In 1977 the German Army announced its order for 1,800 Leopard 2s. Production was split between Krauss-Maffei, Munich and MaK, Kiel, with the first training vehicles being completed in 1978, and the first full Leopard 2 being delivered in 1979.

The Leopard 2 has the same conventional four-man crew layout as the Leopard 1. The driver is positioned in the front right of the hull. In the turret on the centre of the hull the commander sits to the right, with the gunner ahead of him and loader to his left. The engine and transmission are housed at the rear of the hull. The Leopard 2 is fitted with the V-12-cylinder MTU MB-873 Ka-501 diesel engine giving 1,500 hp. This is a larger engine than the 10-cylinder MTU engine fitted to the Leopard 1 but is required to give the heavier Leopard 2 the same mobility as the earlier MBT. (In fact, the top speed of the Leopard 2 is 72 km/h, compared with 65 km/h for the Leopard 1.) The armour of the Leopard 2 has also been upgraded from the all-steel Leopard 1, with the all-welded hull and slab-sided turret being made of Chobham laminate/steel armour.

The Leopard 2 has pioneered the use of the 120 mm smooth-bore gun. Previous Western tanks had used a 105 mm main gun, and the Leopard 2 prototypes trialled both a 105 mm and 120 mm gun, both manufactured by Rheinmetall, before the increased range of the 120 mm gun led to the larger gun being chosen. Two types of 120 mm projectile can be used – APFSDS rounds, and general-purpose HEAT/HE rounds. The gun has powered elevation and traverse and is fitted with an advanced fire-control system, including a combined laser and stereoscopic rangefinder. The gun is also fully stabilised, enabling it to be fired accurately when on the move. A semi-automatic loading mechanism for the bulky ammunition assists the loader. The additional armament of a 7.62 mm MG3 coaxial machine-gun and a second 7.62 mm MG3 anti-aircraft machine-gun fitted to the loader's hatch is the same as on the Leopard 1. Eight smoke grenade dischargers are also fitted on each side of the turret.

Although not tested on the battlefield, the Leopard 2 is regarded as an extremely effective MBT, combining heavy firepower, good armour protection and mobility, as well as having proved reliability through its use of well-tried components and manufacturing technology. As well as being in service in the German Army (the last production vehicles of the **Leopard 2A4** being delivered in 1992) it has been sold to Austria, Denmark, the Netherlands, Spain, Sweden (designated **Stridsvagn 121**) and Switzerland (where it has been constructed under licence by the Federal Construction Works, Thun, and is designated **Pz87 Leo**). There is also an ARV variant known as the **Büffel** (Buffalo), an AVLB variant and a driver-training vehicle variant. All Leopard 2s are also fitted as standard with a full range of night vision equipment and an NBC system.

By the late 1980s the German Army decided that major improvements to the design of the Leopard 2 were needed, and work began on the most important Leopard 2 variant, the **Leopard 2A5**, also known as the **Leopard 2 (Improved)**, with the first prototypes being produced in 1990. In 1994 the German and Dutch armies started a programme of upgrading existing Leopard 2s in service to 2A5 standard. The most obvious visible change is that the front turret on the 2A5 has been reshaped into an arrowhead profile by the addition of new removable panels of armour in order to provide increased protection against kinetic (APFSDS/APDS) and chemical (HEAT) rounds. Additional armoured panels have also been fitted to the skirts to provide extra protection for the suspension and hull sides. The electrical and electronic systems have also been overhauled, with a new navigation system, a new all-electric gun-control system, an upgraded laser rangefinding system, a thermal imaging sight for the commander and a rear-mounted television monitor for the driver when reversing being provided. Other improvements include lining the turret with a spall inhibitor.

A replacement main gun has also been planned for the 2A5 upgrade, although this has not yet been approved. Two new guns are being developed. The first is another 120 mm smooth-bore gun, the L55, built by Rheinmetall but with the muzzle lengthened from .44 to .55 calibres to give an increased muzzle velocity. It will also be able to fire the latest APFSDS-T (Armour Piercing Fin-Stabilised Discarding Sabot – Tracer) armament. When fitted with the L55 gun, the 2A5 will be redesignated the **Leopard 2A6**. A further improved variant, the **2A6 EX**, which will have an auxiliary power unit, is also projected. The second gun being developed is a 140 mm gun with bustle-mounted autoloader, which would reduce the tank's crew to three.

The Leopard 2A5 is also being newly built for the Swedish and Spanish armies. The Swedish tanks are designated **Strv-122**, and as well as the improvements made to the German and Dutch 2A5s, have additional Swedish-developed armour on the front, sides and turret roof, a new laser rangefinder and a Celsius command and control system. Spain's 2A5s are being built under licence and are designated **2A5E** (E = *España*).

*Leopard 2 MBT of the Dutch Army in Bosnia*

## SPECIFICATION:

**Leopard 2**
**Crew:** 4
**Armament:** 1 x 120 mm main gun, 1 x 7.62 mm coaxial machine-gun, 1 x 7.62 mm AA machine-gun, 16 x smoke grenade dischargers
**Ammunition:** 42 rounds, 120 mm; 4,750 rounds, 7.62 mm
**Dimensions:** length (hull) 7.72 m, (including main armament) 9.67 m; height (turret top) 2.48 m; width 3.70 m; ground clearance 0.49 m
**Weight:** loaded 55,150 kg; ground pressure 0.83 kg/cm$^2$
**Engine:** MTU MB-873 Ka-501 12-cylinder liquid-cooled diesel; output 1,500 hp
**Performance:** range 550 km; maximum speed 72 km/h; speed cross-country 50 km/h
**Armour:** steel/laminate

**Leopard 2A5**
**Crew:** 4
**Armament:** 1 x 120 mm main gun, 1 x 7.62 mm coaxial machine-gun, 1 x 7.62 mm AA machine-gun, 16 x smoke grenade dischargers
**Ammunition:** 42 rounds, 120 mm; 4,750 rounds, 7.62 mm
**Dimensions:** length (hull) 7.72 m, (including main armament) 9.97 m; height (turret top) 2.64 m; width 3.74m; ground clearance 0.49 m
**Weight:** loaded 59,700 kg; ground pressure 0.89 kg/cm$^2$
**Engine:** MTU MB-873 Ka-501 12-cylinder liquid-cooled diesel; output 1,500 hp
**Performance:** range 500 km; maximum speed 72 km/h; speed cross-country 50 km/h
**Armour:** steel/laminate

# Leopard Buffalo ARV and Pionierpanzer

*Pionierpanzer 2 Dachs Armoured Combat Engineer Vehicle*

THE LEOPARD 1 MAIN BATTLE TANK was developed by West Germany in the 1950s, initially in conjunction with France and Italy. Although the other two countries pulled out, Germany went ahead with the design, and the first Leopard 1 was delivered to the German Army in 1965. Since then it has become one of the most successful postwar MBT designs with its combination of firepower and mobility, and has been sold throughout the world, still being in service in many countries. A number of variants were also built over the years, including the Armoured Recovery Vehicle (ARV) (also known as the **Bergepanzer Leopard**) and Armoured Engineer Vehicle (AEV) (also known as the **Pionierpanzer Leopard**) specialised support tanks.

The ARV has been developed to repair or recover tanks which have broken down or been disabled on the battlefield. The first prototypes were built in 1966,

with the vehicle put into production by the company MaK, Kiel, the same year, continuing until 1971. The basic Leopard 1 chassis is used, on which is mounted the specialist equipment: a hydraulically operated crane, a main tow winch with a second hoisting winch on the right side of the crew compartment and a dozer blade at the front of the vehicle. An improved version has also been produced which has increased lifting capability and is fitted with a stabilising jack at the vehicle rear. The four-man crew comprises a commander, a driver and two mechanics who carry a range of specialist repair equipment. The vehicle is armed with two 7.62 mm machine-guns, one mounted on the commander's cupola and the other on the hull front next to the glacis plate. The ARV is in service in the German Army, and has also been sold to Australia, Belgium, Canada, Italy, the Netherlands and Norway.

*Bergepanzer 2 Armoured Recovery Vehicle*

The AEV was also built by MaK, Kiel, being produced from 1968 to 1971. Again using the basic Leopard 1 chassis, the specialist engineer vehicle is similar to the ARV in appearance, with a crane and a winch mounted on the hull and a dozer blade (larger than that on the ARV, for heavy-duty continuous bulldozing) with scarifiers mounted at the front of the vehicle. In addition the AEV carries a large earth-auger, which is used to bore foxholes, on the back of the hull. The four-man crew also carry a range of specialist engineering equipment and demolition explosives. The vehicle is armed with two 7.62 mm machine-guns. The Pionierpanzer is in service in the German Army and has also been sold to Belgium, Italy and the Netherlands.

A new ARV, based on the Leopard 2 MBT and called the **Büffel** (Buffalo), has also been built by Krauss-Maffei Wegmann and MaK. The first production Buffalos were delivered in 1991, and the vehicle is in service with the German and Dutch armies, as well as being on order to Spain and Sweden. The Buffalo is fitted with a range of specialised equipment, including a hydraulic crane, winch and stabilising/dozer blade.

## SPECIFICATION:

### ARV
**Crew:** 4
**Armament:** 2 x 7.62 mm machine-guns
**Ammunition:** 3,000 rounds, 7.62 mm
**Dimensions:** length 7.45 m; height 2.70 m; width 3.25 m; ground clearance 0.44 m
**Weight:** empty 39,800 kg; loaded 40,400 kg; ground pressure 0.85 kg/cm$^2$
**Engine:** MTU MB-838 Ka-M500 10-cylinder water-cooled diesel; output 830 hp
**Performance:** range 500 km; maximum speed 62 km/h; speed cross-country 40 km/h
**Armour:** steel – 35 mm front, 25–30 mm sides, 25 mm rear

### AEV
**Crew:** 4
**Armament:** 2 x 7.62 mm machine-guns
**Ammunition:** 3,000 rounds, 7.62 mm
**Dimensions:** length 7.88 m; height 2.70 m; width 3.25 m; ground clearance 0.44 m
**Weight:** empty 40,800 kg; loaded 41,400 kg; ground pressure 0.87 kg/cm$^2$
**Engine:** MTU MB-838 Ka-M500 10-cylinder water-cooled diesel; output 830 hp
**Performance:** range 800 km; maximum speed 62 km/h; speed cross-country 40 km/h
**Armour:** steel – 35 mm front, 25–30 mm sides, 25 mm rear

# Luchs A2 Light Tank/Amphibious Recce Vehicle

*Spähpanzer Luchs or Lynx*

ORIGINALLY DEVELOPED AND MANUFACTURED by Rheinstahl Wehrtechnik, now Henschel Wehrteknik GmbH, a part of Rheinmetall DeTec AG, the **Luchs** is an armoured amphibious reconnaissance vehicle with an 8 x 8 configuration capable of carrying a wide variety of weapons systems with or without a turret. The heavier main gun variants have the spaced armour Rheinmetall TS-7 turret in the centre of the hull, mounted with either a 120 mm or 105 mm gun or a 20 mm cannon, as well as a turret machine-gun capable of being operated either manually or automatically. The commander and gunner are seated side by side in the centre of the vehicle, with the commander to the left, the driver up front of them and the radio-operator on the left at the back. All these areas are hatched and periscoped. A main entrance hatch is located on the left side of the hull between the sets of wheels. The engine is in its own compartment at the back on the right, behind the turret, separated from the crew's compartment by gas-tight welded bulkheads and fitted with an automatic fire-suppression system. The engine itself is rigged to be easily extractable and can be operated outside the vehicle. Using a four-speed hydraulic torque converter via a distributor gear with differential locks to the wheels, the Luchs has the same power and speed capability whether travelling forwards or backwards. It is also fully amphibious, equipped with internal bulkheads and powered using two Schottel steerable propellers sited underneath the hull. Its watertight integrity combines with its NBC capability,

both of which are to a very high standard and enhance this vehicle's survivability. The upgrades to the original vehicle have been the **Luchs A1**, fitted with SEM 80/90 radio, and the current **Luchs A2**, fitted with thermal night vision equipment, a GPS navigation system including gyrocompass, an updated NBC suite and still more sensor equipment.

---

## SPECIFICATION:

**Crew:** 4

**Armament:** Variants: Rheinmetall 120 mm smooth-bore gun, 105 mm gun, or 20 mm Mk 20 Rh 202 cannon, a Rheinmetall 7.62 mm MG3 machine-gun, or a range of other weapons, including missiles and anti-aircraft guns

**Ammunition:** relative to variant weapons systems mounted.

**Dimensions:** length 6.203 m; height 2.083 m (without turret); width 2.98 m; ground clearance 0.45 m

**Weight:** empty 17,300 kg; loaded 24,500 kg; ground pressure 17.75 kg/cm²

**Engine:** diesel; output 435 hp

**Performance:** range 1,000 km; maximum speed 115 km/h; speed cross-country 60–80 km/h

**Armour:** plate steel

# M1/ M1A1/ M1A2 Abrams MBT

*Abrams M1 MBT*

THE AMERICAN **ABRAMS M1** PROGRAM began in 1971, searching for a radical new tank to replace the somewhat outmoded US MBTs of that time. Since the first prototypes the basic design has undergone improvements and upgrades until there are now currently some five versions in service with the US Army, though there is an attempt to standardise them all with the latest upgrade.

In 1973 Chrysler won a competition for the prototype contract against a rival bid from the General Motors Corporation, and work began at its Detroit Arsenal Tank Plant in 1978, with the first tanks operational by 1982. In the same year Chrysler sold off its tank-building subsidiary to General Dynamics. By May 1985 2,380 M1s had been produced, when production was then switched to the **Improved M1**, or **IPM1**, an interim model between the M1 and the **M1A1**, featuring improved turret and frontal armour. Almost 1,000 of the IPM1 were built before a further upgrade was introduced: the M1A1.

The M1A1 was also initially built at the Detroit Arsenal Tank Plant until 1991, when final assembly switched to the Lima Army Tank Plant in Ohio. The Detroit plant then closed down completely in 1996. By this time 7,467 M1s and upgrades had been delivered.

The M1A1 was substantially different from its original. As well as the IPM1 upgraded armour, it had a new main armament – a 120 mm smooth-bore gun called M256, the American designation for the German Rheinmetall MBT main armament used on their Leopard series. It also had a radical new integrated NBC system, increased shock aborption, modified transmission and other internal upgrades and development tweaks too numerous to mention. The first M1A1 was completed in 1984 and delivered in 1986, with a total of 4,796 delivered up to 1993. There was also a heavier variant, the M1A1 with DU armour. Announced in 1988 and released later that year, it had a still newer armour protection upgrade

*Abrams M1A2 MBT*

featuring steel-encased depleted uranium, possessing a density two and a half times that of its steel equivalent and weighing in at around 65 tons. These upgrades were shipped to the active service units within the NATO area of operations – an aim that has been consistently followed by the US Army, so that its front-line armour is of the latest, most up-to-date manufacture.

By 1993 production of the M1A1 gave way to the latest in the M1 series upgrades: the **M1A2**. Though the external features of this version have remained pretty much the same as the M1A1 variant, the inside design and equipment have been radically upgraded and renewed. This includes more engines tweaks, an improved commander's weapons control station and independent thermal viewer, an inter-vehicle information system, a GPS navigation system and increased protection and survival initiatives installed throughout the internal specifications.

The M1 and its upgrades have hull and turrets heavily armoured with Chobham composite armour for increased protection, with the crew compartment also separated from the fuel tanks by internal armoured bulkheads, along with complete internal protective fire-suppression systems. The four-man crew consists of a driver in a semi-reclined position at the front centre of the tank with a hatch and periscopes, including night-driving image intensification; the commander and gunner are situated on the right side of the turret, with the loader on the left. The fire-control system consists of a laser rangefinder, full-solution solid state digital computer and a stabilised day and night thermal sight, permitting accurate fire whether stationary or moving. All this is automated with manual input for the sight range, ammunition type and temperature, and muzzle compensation.

The Lycoming Textron AGT 1500 gas turbine

*Abrams M1A1 MBT*

engine has excellent acceleration and behavioural characteristics, but this awesome power is heavy on fuel consumption. This is compounded by the fact that there is no back-up system or auxiliary power unit (APU), and so the tank must keep its main engine running, even when stationary, to power the weapons and essential life systems on board – further increasing fuel consumption.

The Ohio Lima plant is now also upgrading older M1s and M1A1s to the M1A2 configuration. The M1 upgrade features a new turret on an upgraded chassis. The M1A2 is also being marketed abroad, especially in the Middle East, with Egypt and Saudi Arabia having already bought the tank and other countries expressing interest.

Today there is also the M1A2 SEP (Systems Enhancement Package), which is designed to bring all Abrams versions up to a consistent level and a single configuration. This system is also designed to take into account further design tweaks and upgrade initiatives. There is also a version of the M1A2 fitted with a fuel-efficient diesel power-pack (the IDPP) in place of its gas turbine power-plant, developed for the export market. Further engine research has been carried out as the AGT 1500 engine is no longer in production – though stockpiles are kept. Apart from the IDPP, other power-plants, including the LV100 Advanced Propulsion System and the Condor CV-12, are currently being considered.

## SPECIFICATION:

### M1/IPM1
**Crew:** 4
**Armament:** 105 mm M68 rifled gun, 1 x 7.62 mm co-axial machine-gun, 1 x 12.7 mm anti-aircraft machine-gun on commander's cupola, 1 x 7.62 mm anti-aircraft machine-gun on loader's hatch
**Ammunition:** 55 rounds (main); 11,400 rounds, 7.62 mm; 1,000 rounds, 12.7 mm; 24 smoke grenades
**Dimensions:** length (hull) 7.918 m, (gun forward) 9.766 m; height 2.885 m; width 3.653 m; ground clearance 0.432 m
**Weight:** loaded 54,545 kg; ground pressure 0.96 kg/cm$^2$
**Engine:** gas turbine; output 1,500 hp
**Performance:** range 498 km; maximum speed 72.42 km/h; speed cross-country 48.3 km/h
**Armour:** Chobham composite armour, exact make-up classified

### M1A1/M1A2
**Crew:** 4
**Armament:** 120 mm M256 smooth-bore main gun, 1 x 7.62 mm co-axial machine-gun, 1 x 12.7 mm anti-aircraft machine-gun on commander's cupola, 1 x 7.62 mm anti-aircraft machine-gun on loader's hatch
**Ammunition:** 40 rounds (main); 12,400 rounds, 7.62mm; 1,000 rounds, 12.7mm; 24 smoke grenades
**Dimensions:** length (hull) 7.918 m, (gun forward) 9.828 m; height 2.886 m; width 3.657 m; ground clearance 0.432 m
**Weight:** loaded 57,154 kg; ground pressure 0.96 kg/cm$^2$
**Engine:** gas turbine; output 1,500 hp
**Performance:** range 498 km; maximum speed 66.77 km/h; speed cross-country 48.3 km/h
**Armour:** Chobham composite armour, exact make-up classified

# M109A6 Paladin SP Artillery

*M109A6 Paladin 155 mm self-propelled howitzer*

THE **M109A6** SP HOWITZER is part of the 109 series with a long and distinguished service career with the US Army, stretching back to the 1960s. Indeed for so long has it been a front-line weapon that it is now more numerous than any other type of SP howitzer, and it has been exported to many other countries all over the world. The **A6 Paladin** variant was chosen after many programmes for new howitzers and initiatives to prolong the life of existing SP artillery were finally boiled down, with the M109 settled on as the gun most worthy of upgrading – an upgrade path which continues to this day.

Thus in 1985 BMY Combat Systems was awarded the initial development contract (along with Israeli partners) and came up with various prototypes which were tested from 1988 to 1989. From this the US Army chose the 109A6, which went into initial production in 1990, the first versions being available

from 1992. BMY went on to produce 164 M109A6 Paladins up until the end of 1994. The rest of the order was then put out to tender again, this time being won by the FMC Corporation. The specifics of the order were to upgrade some 60 existing M109s and to build some 650 systems afresh. In 1997 the US Army turned to yet another different manufacturer – United Defense – to supply an additional 40 M109A6s with an upgraded chassis supplied by Letterkenny Army Depot. The United Defense provenance is the manufacture of the turret and its integration with the supplied chassis, with various options offered with a view to the export market, such as a change of power-pack and a semi-automatic loader.

The A6's main gun is the M284 cannon – itself a modified M185 gun with a total upgrade. The barrel, along with the rest of the gun mechanisms, has been

upgraded and modified, with some sections being completely redesigned. Its rate of fire is four rounds a minute for three minutes followed by one round per minute for an hour. The turret's and gun's traverse are both hydraulic and hand powered, and it can handle all types of ordnance, including chemical and nuclear shells. Rocket-assisted rounds have still further increased its range to over 30,000 metres. With its computer-controlled fire-control system and modified main armament, the power and accuracy of the M109A6 Paladin has improved constantly.

By reducing the crew size from six to four, more room and comfort has been provided internally. The driver sits at the front of the hull with the engine on his right, and the other three crew members – commander, gunner and loader – are all located in the gun turret itself.

Through these upgrades all aspects of the original M109 SP howitzer have been improved, with performance increases across the board: in computer power, rate of fire, accuracy, survivability, all-round reliability, NBC capability, and crew protection. This upgrade path continues, with system improvement packages continuing to be introduced. The M109A Paladin has been chosen for both the US Army and the National Guard and is deployed in batteries of six. It also continues to fill export order-books.

*The Israeli Defence Forces are one of the main users of the M109 SP artillery system and have upgraded their vehicles under the name of Doher*

## SPECIFICATION:

**Crew:** 4
**Armament:** main guns: 1 x 155 mm M284 howitzer main gun, 1 x 12.7 mm M2 machine-gun (anti-aircraft)
**Ammunition:** 39 rounds, main gun; 500 rounds, 12.7 mm
**Dimensions:** overall length 9.677 m; height 3.62 m; width 3.149 m; ground clearance 0.457 m
**Weight:** loaded 28,849 kg; ground pressure 0.951 kg/cm$^2$
**Engine:** Detroit Diesel 8V-71T LHR; output 440 bhp at 2,300 rpm
**Performance:** range 344 km; maximum speed 64.4 km/h
**Armour:** 25 mm steel

# M113 Family APC/AIFV

*An M113 fitters vehicle in service in Bosnia*

IN AN UNUSUAL DISPLAY OF LONGEVITY for military hardware, the **M113** family stretches back over 40 years to the time of its original introduction. In fact there are more versions and variants around today than ever before, making it the most widely used military vehicle in the world, with over 80,000 built in the USA and also under licence in Italy. The M113 was the first aluminium Armoured Fighting Vehicle (AFV) to be built and is currently used in over fifty countries worldwide. Its versatility in military operations has made this slab-sided, tracked APC a leader in its field. This versatility is amply demonstrated by the number of variants and separate uses to which the vehicle has been allocated.

The first prototype of the M113 was built in the late 1950s, following an Army requirement for a new air-transportable APC. Originally designated **T113** for the aluminium hull and **T117** for its potential steel counterpart, the aluminium version was finally chosen and redesignated M113. Production began in 1960 at the San José FMC plant in California. The first versions were operational by 1962/3. In 1964 the first upgrade, designated **M113A1**, was produced, having a longer range because of its new diesel engine, which replaced the earlier petrol version. The next upgrade came in 1979 with the **M113A2**, which featured a complete engine and suspension overhaul, along with increased ground clearance. In 1987 came

*M113A3 APC with add-on armour kit*

Potential exists even for civil deployment, with specialist fire-fighting, hazardous material, accident and recovery vehicle variants. Other nations have also adapted the M113 family to suit a variety of climates, terrains and requirements.

In 1992 production ceased at the San José plant, ostensibly for good. However, many continuing foreign orders have resurrected the production of the M113 family. The US Army also continues to use this workhorse, and its 17,500 fleet in current use will remain for the foreseeable future. Therefore upgrade paths and packages will be maintained and new ones introduced for a patriotic motive quite besides the extraordinary success of the M113 family as a lucrative export for the USA.

the **M113A3** kit upgrade, featuring the General Motors Detroit turbo-charged diesel 6V-53T engine, updated transmission and suspension, and different driver's controls, extra exterior fuel tanks and an add-on armour suite. This upgrade system is known as RISE (Reliability Improved Selected Equipment), and all M113s modified by this power train package have been redesignated to A3 nomenclature.

The basic version has a two-man crew consisting of a driver and commander, and an infantry compartment at the rear of the vehicle with room to hold eleven men and their equipment, or cargo or another weapons system. Entry to this rear compartment is from a ramp door at the rear, though there is also an access roof hatch. The driver is positioned on the left at the front of the hull, with the engine beside him on the right. The commander is seated more centrally behind the engine compartment with his own fully rotating cupola above, with the 12.7 mm Browning machine-gun attached.

As well as being air-transportable, the vehicle is fully amphibious – propelled by the rotation of its tracks. Further versatility is obtained by using the interior space for an almost limitless variety of functions. A relevant criticism of the M113 family is that today its speed has been surpassed by current battlefield MBTs and other vehicles such as the M2 Bradley Infantry Fighting Vehicle (IFV); but there is still very much a place for these vehicles in a myriad of other military roles – some of which are explained by the variant listings. Different interior models are tailored for different functions, which include: bulldozer; cargo or infantry carrier; ambulance; command post; anti-aircraft/anti-tank/missile: ADATS/TOW/SAM; mortar; specialist smoke; mine-layer; maintenance/recovery; fire support; recce; OpFor surrogate (approximating opposing armies' equivalent equipment); light tank.

All these various functions have their own suites of equipment that are custom installed into the basic hull, although there are even stretched variants. These have a longer wheelbase in order to increase and enhance the internal space by providing room for more equipment and personnel.

*Canadian Army M113A2 engineering variant specially equipped vehicle with dozer blade and earth auger*

## SPECIFICATION:

**Crew:** according to variant; standard 2 plus 11 infantry
**Armament:** 1 x 12.7 mm M2 machine-gun or 1 x 7.62 mm machine-gun
**Ammunition:** 1–2,000 rounds
**Dimensions:** length 9.677 m; height 3.62 m; width 3.149 m; ground clearance 0.43 m
**Weight:** unloaded 9,630–11,270 kg; loaded 11,070–12,150 kg according to variant; ground pressure 0.54–0.57 kg/cm$^2$
**Engine:** General Motors Detroit Diesel 6V-53; output 275 hp at 2,800 rpm
**Performance:** range 480 km; maximum speed 64.4 km/h; range 485 km
**Armour:** aluminium, with some upgrades having an option of steel appliquéd armour

# M2 and M3 APC/AIFV

WHEN THE SOVIETS INTRODUCED THEIR BMP IFV in 1967, NATO forces had nothing equivalent that could match it, as the M113 APC lacked its speed and punch, so development of a new IFV was considered of paramount importance. In 1972 after a considerable gap, filled with upgrades of existing vehicles and unsuccessful prototypes, came the prototype **XM723**, which went on to become in 1978 the **M2/M3** series, made by the FMC Corporation (now United Defense LP), the same company that made the M113 family of vehicles. Following Army recommendations, partly due to economic restraints, a common vehicle was developed for an IFV, the M2, and a cavalry reconnaissance vehicle, the M3. Both vehicles are based on the same chassis and have slightly different suites fitted according to their purpose. The M2 is designed to allow the infantry to fight under armour from within the vehicle, as well as to transport them swiftly and keep up with the faster modern main battle tanks and combat vehicles. Thus the main advantages that the M2/M3 have over the M113 series are increased mobility and speed, greater firepower and better protection. With an anti-tank capability provided by the TOW ATGW mounted on the opposite side to the main armament, the M2 packs a punch that upgrades the infantry which it also transports.

*Bradley M2A2 IFV with appliqué passive armour fitted to hull and turret*

The first prototype versions of the M2 IFV were delivered to the US Army in 1978/9, and after comprehensive testing orders were made in the early 1980s for some 500 vehicles. Also from 1981 onwards the M2/M3 series was named after General Omar Bradley as the **Bradley FV**.

In 1991 the US Army ordered a further 1,600 Bradleys, and by 1995, when the last vehicles rolled off the production line, some 6,800 had been built. Now research is currently being carried out into the future infantry fighting vehicle, but meanwhile the Bradley's operational life has been extended with a variant and upgrade path which will prolong its front-line life considerably. Its performance in the Gulf War was exemplary, where it out-performed any enemy infantry vehicles while maintaining a high record for reliability in all its systems.

Like the M113 series, the Bradley is air-transportable, made from aluminium with appliquéd steel plate armour added onto the front of the hull, the side skirts, the rear and the turret. The driver's seat is on the left at the front of the hull, with a periscoped

*A Bradley M2A3 IFV fires a TOW ATGW missile*

hatch complete with night vision facility. The engine compartment is also in the front, to the right. The turret is centrally mounted, with the gunner to the left and the commander to the right, and equipped with primary and secondary sights and periscopes. The main armament is the Boeing M242 25 mm Bushmaster chain gun with a dual feed (older versions sported the 25 mm Hughes chain gun) and there is a 7.62 mm M240C machine-gun mounted coaxially with it. On the other side of the turret is a dual pod of TOW ATGWs. There are also smoke grenade launchers mounted on either side of the two-man turret.

The rear has room to hold seven infantrymen (in the case of the **M2A2** only six) including the commander, with access via a ramp door at the back of the vehicle. There is also a rear hatch on the roof. There are a further six firing ports, each with its own integral periscope, two on either side of the hull and two in the rear (the M2A2 lacks the hull side ports). All M2/M3s and their variants (M2A1/M2A2/M3A1/M3A2) have excellent amphibious capabilities enhanced with an erectible water barrier, with their tracks providing propulsion.

The variant and upgrades to the basic model all come with improved suspension and NBC capability, GPS navigation systems, missile countermeasures,

TOW, and better night sights and thermal imaging. Armour has been further increased, along with better internal fire-suppression systems. These include versions with explosive reactive armour (ERA), a command vehicle, MLRS (multiple launch rocket system), a medi-vac ambulance, fire control, support, anti-aircraft.

### SPECIFICATION:

**Crew:** 3 crew and 6 infantry
**Armament:** 1 x Boeing M242 25 mm Bushmaster chain gun or 1 x 25 mm Hughes chain gun, 1 x 7.62 mm coaxial machine-gun, launcher for 2 x TOW ATGWs
**Dimensions:** length 6.45 m; height 2.97 m; width 3.20 m; ground clearance 0.432 m
**Weight:** 22,680 kg; ground pressure 0.54 kg/cm$^2$
**Engine:** Cummins VTA-903T diesel; output 506 hp
**Performance:** range 480 km; maximum speed 66 km/h
**Armour:** aluminium with steel appliquéd armour added to the front hull and turret

# TURKEY
# M60A3 MBT

**A**S SAID IN THE MAGACH-8 ENTRY, THE **M48/M60** series was one of the giants of the postwar world, equipping the armies of many nations. Even today a vast number remain in service – 1,500 with Egypt, 1,350 with Israel, and nearly 1,000 with Turkey, who had also taken the earlier M48A3 in quantity – nearly 3,000. Turkey's vehicles are either M60A1s (around 275) or **M60A3s** with a TTS (Tank Thermal Sight). All came from the US Army.

Chrysler started building the M60 family in 1960, and had developed three main variants before the M60A3 – the original M60, the M60A1 which had a new turret, and the M60A2 armed with the Shillelagh 152 mm gun/missile system. The M60A3 had many improvements over the older versions, and in the early 1980s, by which time the M60A1 production line had ceased, it was the most advanced American MBT in service. It had stabilisation of its main armament – the M68 rifled 105 mm – in both elevation and traverse; an air cleaner; gunner's thermal sight; improved searchlight; AVDS-1790-2C Reliability Improved Selected Equipment (RISE) engine; a thermal sleeve for the main gun; a Raytheon laser rangefinder; an improved coaxial weapon; smoke dischargers on both turret sides; and an engine smoke generator.

The M60A3 has seen a lot of action over the years, mainly at the hands of the Israelis, although it was also used in the Gulf (by Saudi Arabia) and by the Iranians in the Iran–Iraq war during the 1980s; often photographs of M60s in service show additional features such as mine ploughs, mine rollers, dozer blades, etc. The US Army worried a lot about how effective the M60 was in comparison to its anticipated foe, principally the Soviet T-72. The M60A1 was supposed not to be its equal; the M60A3 was said to

*The M60A3 remains one of the most numerous MBTs in the world*

be better. In the end, as is so often the case, the real answer lay in the proficiency of the crews. Certainly in the Gulf War the M60A1s of the US 1st Marine Division accounted for over 50 T-72s without problems.

There were two other versions of the M60 family – the AVLB (bridgelayer) which launched an aluminium scissors bridge, and the M728 Combat Engineer Vehicle (see next entry).

---

## SPECIFICATION:

**Crew:** 4

**Armament:** 105 mm M68 rifled gun (main), 7.62 mm machine-gun (coaxial), 12.7 mm machine-gun (anti-aircraft)

**Ammunition:** 63 rounds, main gun; 6,000 rounds, 7.62 mm; 900 rounds, 12.7 mm

**Dimensions:** length 9.436 m; height 3.27 m; width 3.631 m; ground clearance 0.45 m

**Weights:** empty 48,684 kg; loaded/combat 52,617 kg; ground pressure 0.87 kg/cm$^2$

**Engine:** AVDS-1790-2C, General Dynamics Land Systems (formerly Continental)

**Performance:** road speed – max. 48.28 km/h; speed cross-country 35 km/h

**Armour:** no details officially published

---

# M728 Combat Engineer Vehicle

*M728 Combat Engineer Vehicle*

The **M728 CEV** was designed in the 1960s under the designation **T118E1**, entering production in 1965 and US Army service in 1968. Over 300 were built, the majority remaining in US service, although a few went to Saudi Arabia and Singapore. Armed with a 165 mm M135 demolition gun with a short barrel, it also carries a coaxially mounted 7.62 mm machine-gun and a commander's 12.7 mm machine-gun. Other equipment includes a frontally mounted hydraulic dozer blade; an A-frame that can fold over the back of the turret; a 11,340 kg capacity winch; and an infra-red searchlight mounted over the M135 gun. Now long in the tooth, the M728 is to be replaced by the Grizzly, based on the M1 Abrams chassis.

### SPECIFICATION:

**Crew:** 4 (commander, gunner, loader, driver)
**Armament:** 165 mm main gun, 7.62 mm coaxial machine-gun, 12.7 mm commander's machine-gun
**Weights:** loaded 52,163 kg
**Armour:** n/a

# M110 SP Artillery

THE US ARMY OF THE 1950s NEEDED air-portable mobile artillery, and the Pacific Car and Foundry Company was awarded the contract to produce a range of prototypes. Tests led to contracts for the M107 (175 mm) and the **M110** (203 mm) in 1961. The first production vehicles entered service in the early 1960s, and production of the original M110 was completed (after some 750 vehicles) by the end of the decade. The M107 and M110 were phased out (many were upgraded) with the arrival in service in 1977 of the **M110A1** and, subsequently in the 1980s, the **M110A2**. The M110A1 has a longer M201 203 mm gun, which allows larger charges to be used and therefore provides an increased muzzle velocity and range to 22,900 m from the 16,800 m of the M110's M2A2. Main ammunition for both guns was the M106 HE and M404 anti-personnel rounds.

In 1978 the M110A2 was standardised. It is an M110A1 with an improved muzzle brake and improved range. As well as the M106 and M404 rounds, the M110A2 can also fire the M509A1 Improved Conventional Munition (180 anti-personnel grenades). In British and US hands it also has the capability to fire nuclear shells.

Used by the US Army, and the armies of Bahrain* (from USA and the Netherlands), Belgium, Germany, Greece (from USA and Germany)*, Great Britain, Iran*, Israel, Italy*, Japan (manufactured under licence)*, Jordan (from USA)*, Morocco (from USA)*, the Netherlands, Pakistan*, Spain (from USA)*, South Korea*, Taiwan* and Turkey (from USA and Germany)*, the M110 is still in service in Israel, Iran and South Korea. (M110A2 users are indicated by an asterisk in the list above, the main holders

*The M110 self-propelled artillery system was first used in combat during the Vietnam War and remains in widespread use worldwide*

being Greece and Turkey.) The USA keeps a number of M110A2s in reserve.

The M110 is an exceptional weapon with a good reputation for accuracy and mobility. Its 13-man crew includes eight carried in the support/ammunition-carrying vehicle (**M548** or **FV623 Stalwart**); only the driver is under armour in his position at the front of the vehicle to the left of the engine. The British Army made use of its M110A2s in the Gulf War, but later phased them out to make room for the MLRS.

## SPECIFICATION:

**Crew:** 13 (5 in vehicle; rest in M548 support vehicle)
**Armament:** 203 mm M2A2 howitzer main gun (M110A2 – M201)
**Ammunition:** 2 rounds
**Dimensions:** length 7.467 m; height 2.93 m; width 3.149 m; ground clearance 0.44 m
**Weights:** empty 24,312 kg; loaded 26,534 kg; ground pressure 0.76 kg/cm$^2$
**Engine:** Detroit Diesel turbo-charged 2-stroke, liquid-cooled 8-cylinder, output 405 hp
**Performance:** range 725 km; road speed 56 km/h; fording capability 1.066 m
**Armour:** n/a

# M270 MLRS

*The M270 multiple launch rocket system was used by both the US and British armies to devastating effect during the Gulf War of 1991*

THE **M270** MULTIPLE LAUNCH ROCKET SYSTEM (MLRS) gained much exposure on television at the time of the Gulf War, thanks to the strong televisual appeal of multiple launches lighting up a night sky. Whether its effectiveness was war-winning, as some US commanders said, or whether it was simply a 'grid square remover' as the men on the ground nicknamed it, the multiple launch rocket system has become an important part of the US and Western Allies' inventory. Its ability to saturate a given area with a sophisticated array of multiple munitions that divide from the larger rockets fired from the main pod makes its firepower awesomely effective.

The story of the M270 started in the mid-1970s when US Army Missile Command began feasibility studies. Five companies (among them Boeing and eventual prime contractor the Vought Corporation) were awarded contracts to produce studies for what was then called the General Support Rocket System.

The winner, for what had become a standard NATO weapon, the MLRS, was announced: Vought (now Lockheed Martin Missiles and Fire Control – Dallas). In 1983 the M270 reached US Army units and immediately proved to be a reliable and efficient system, a fact borne out by the interest elsewhere. In Europe a consortium of France, Germany, Italy and the UK built the MLRS, the first units being available in 1989. Altogether some 300 were built by the European syndicate, complete with 200,000 rockets of M77 and AT2 calibre.

The M270 has a crew of three, all carried in the front cab, although this sophisticated weapon system can be operated *in extremis* by a single person. The fire-control system has a GPS navigation suite allowing quick targeting. Based on the M2/M3 Bradley IFV chassis, the M270 is a lightly armoured launch vehicle that carries two pre-loaded rocket containers, each of six rockets. Resupply vehicles

vary from country to country, the USA using the Heavy Expanded Mobility Ammunition Trailer (HEMAT) and the UK a system on a Leyland medium mobility load carrier. The MLRS can fire a practice round – the M28A1 – or the M77 rocket, which can carry the M26 dual-purpose anti-personnel/anti-matériel bomblets or AT2 anti-armour submunitions. Under development are more sophisticated terminally guided anti-tank submunitions and a guided rocket (GMLRS is an international project between the European consortium and the USA). The USA has also produced a longer-range variant (used successfully in the Gulf), the TACMS (Army Tactical Missile System), with a range of over 60 km (as opposed to the 31,600 m of the M270), which is fired from a modified M270 but the same fire-control system.

The MLRS is in service with Bahrain, Denmark, France, Germany, Greece, Israel, Italy, Japan, South Korea, the Netherlands, Norway, Turkey, the UK and the USA. Well over 1,200 have been supplied, nearly 300 from the European consortium, the biggest customers being the USA with over 800 launchers, and Germany with 150.

There is also an upgrade path for the M270 launcher, a contract awarded by the US government to the same companies that manufacture the original. Begun in 1998, the enhanced upgrade, the **M270A1**, restores each M270 launcher to a pristine condition, as well as upgrading its fire-control and launch systems, all of which reduce firing times considerably. Other enhancements include a GPS navigation system. The European manufacturers of the MLRS have instigated the development and manufacture of their own enhancements, including a new fire-control system. Israel has also modified the MLRS to fire its own munitions – the LAR 160 and the MAR 350 rockets.

Further upgrades and developments, especially with the munitions fired by the MLRS – its versatility proved by the modifications carried out by a number of countries (M26 warhead, XR-M77 and Guided [GMLRS], ATACMS, MSTAR, BAT, etc.) – are ensuring that this weapons system will have an active life that extends well into the 21st century.

---

## SPECIFICATION:

**Crew:** 3 or 4
**Armament:** rockets in pallets of 6
**Ammunition:** 3.96 m rocket, 227 mm diameter, range 30,000 m (also other variants: M26 warhead, XR-M77 and Guided (GMLRS), ATACMS, MSTAR, BAT, etc.)
**Dimensions:** length (travelling) 6.972 m, (elevated) 5.925 m; height (travelling) 2.6 m, (elevated) 6.97 m; width 2.97 m; ground clearance 0.43 m
**Weight:** empty 20,189 kg; loaded 25,191 kg
**Engine:** Cummins turbo-charged 8-cylinder diesel; output 500 hp
**Performance:** range 483 km; road speed 64 km/h; fording capability 1.1 m

# GERMANY
# Marder APC/AIFV

*Marder 1 A3 AIFV*

WHEN THE WEST GERMAN ARMY was re-formed in the 1950s, a chassis was developed, based upon a Swiss design, that could be used for a number of different purposes. These included the Jagdpanzer Kanone, armed with a 90 mm gun, the Jagdpanzer Rakete, armed with SS.12 ATGWs, and an Infantry Combat Vehicle (ICV) that would develop into the **Marder**. After extensive testing and a number of different prototypes, one of the ICVs was decided on by the West German Army and called the **Marder Schützenpanzer Neu M-1966**. The first production vehicles were delivered to the army in 1970 and production continued until 1975, in all over 3,000 vehicles being produced. The **Marder 1** was to have been supplemented by the **Marder 2**, however, this project was cancelled after only one prototype had been produced.

The all-welded steel hull of the Marder provides its crew with complete protection from small-arms fire and shell splinters, whilst the front of the vehicle is additionally protected against 20 mm projectiles. The layout of the interior is fairly conventional. The driver is seated front left, with one infantryman to his rear and the engine to his right. The two-man turret is in the centre of the vehicle, with the troop compartment to the rear. The infantry debus from the vehicle via a ramp at the back of the hull.

The armament carried by the Marder consists of an externally mounted 20 mm Rheinmetall Mk 20 Rh 202 cannon, along with a 7.62 mm machine-gun mounted coaxially. There are also six smoke grenade dischargers to the left of the cannon. Some Marders

have been fitted with the MILAN ATGW launcher to enable them to engage MBTs to a range of 2,000 m. Also there is a remote-controlled 7.62 mm machine-gun mounted above the rear troop compartment.

There are a wide number of Marder variants in service, including the Roland SAM system, of which over 140 have been built. The chassis of the vehicle also provides the basis for the Argentinian TAM medium tank.

## SPECIFICATION:

**Crew:** 9
**Armament:** 20 mm Mk 20 Rh 202 cannon main gun, 7.62 mm coaxial machine-gun
**Ammunition:** 1,250 rounds main; 5,000 rounds, 7.62 mm
**Dimensions:** length 6.79 m; width 3.24 m; ground clearance 0.44 m
**Weight:** empty 28,200 kg; loaded 29,207 kg
**Engine:** 600 hp at 2,200 rpm
**Performance:** range 520 km; max. road speed 75 km/h
**Armour:** complete protection from small-arms fire and shell splinters. The front of the vehicle gives complete protection against 20 mm projectiles

79

# Merkava MBT

*Merkava Mk 2 MBT*

THE YOM KIPPUR WAR OF 1973 DEVASTATED the Israeli Defence Forces in general and the Armoured Corps in particular, as nearly 1,500 of the IDF's 2,500 dead had been tank soldiers. It was with this as the background that Israel started the development of a new main battle tank. The **Merkava** was the innovative Israeli design of Major-General Israel Tal, one of Israel's most decorated tank soldiers.

The primary design criterion of the Merkava is crew survivability. Every part of the overall design is expected to contribute to helping the crew survive. The engine is in the front to provide protection to the crew. There is a special protective umbrella for the tank commander to enable protection from indirect fire with the hatches open. Special 'spaced armour' is in use along with protected fuel and ammunition compartments. Rear ammunition stowage is combined with a rear entrance and exit. Since the rounds are stowed in containers that can be removed from the vehicle whenever necessary, this space can accommodate tank crewmen who have been forced to abandon their vehicles, or, if thought to be appropriate, even infantrymen. Rear ammunition stowage

allows replenishment much more easily than if rounds have to be replaced in a carousel in the hull centre, as in typical Russian vehicles. The rear entrance and exit to the Merkava also allow the crew to exit the vehicle with a certain degree of protection should the need arise. The Merkava can also carry a small infantry squad internally under complete armoured protection. The main armament of the tank is a M68 105 mm calibre gun, and the tank can carry as many as 92 rounds of main gun ammunition, considerably more than other MBTs of its generation, giving it a strong tactical advantage on the battlefield. The ammunition consists of the M111 and M413 APDS rounds made by Israeli industries. In addition to the main gun, the Merkava carries a 7.62 mm machine-gun mounted coaxially, two 7.62 mm machine-guns on the turret roof, a 60 mm mortar and a 12.7 mm machine-gun mounted over the gun barrel. The turret control system is electrohydraulic.

The principal drawback with the Merkava has been the lack of an adequate power-plant. Initially this was the Teledyne Continental AVDS-1790-6A V-12 diesel 900 hp engine, though this was later replaced

*Merkava Mk 3 MBT*

with a General Dynamics Land Systems power-plant. Both these engines are somewhat underpowered for a tank of over 62 tons. However, one advantage of the location of the engine is that it gives the tank much greater traction, enabling it to climb a 70 per cent gradient, whereas most other MBTs of the period have only been able to manage gradients of 60 per cent.

The first **Merkava Mk 1** tanks were supplied to the IDF in 1979 and received their baptism of fire in Lebanon in 1982, in a campaign which proved the vehicle to be an astounding success, but also highlighted certain areas where improvement was desirable, particularly in the protection to the rear of the vehicle. These defects were corrected with the introduction of the **Mk 2** from 1983 onwards.

## SPECIFICATION:

**Crew:** 4
**Armament:** 105 mm main gun, 7.62 mm coaxial machine-gun, 2 x 7.62 mm machine-guns, 60 mm mortar
**Ammunition:** 62–85 rounds main gun; 10,000 rounds coaxial/anti-aircraft
**Dimensions:** length 8.63 m; height 2.75 m; width 3.7 m; ground clearance 0.47 m
**Weight:** empty 58,000 kg; loaded 60,000 kg; ground pressure 0.9 kg/cm$^2$
**Engine:** General Dynamics Land Systems (formerly Teledyne Continental) AVDS-1790-6A V-12; output 900 hp
**Performance:** range 400 km; road speed 46 km/h
**Armour:** all-round spaced armour

SWITZERLAND
# MOWAG Piranha APC/AIFV

ORIGINALLY DESIGNED by MOWAG of Switzerland
in the late 1960s, the **Piranha** family of light
armoured vehicles, available in 4 x 4, 6 x 6, 8 x 8 and
10 x 10 configurations, has become the choice of
military customers around the world. In 1977 the
Canadian Forces selected the Piranha 6 x 6 Armoured
Vehicle General Purpose (AVGP), using the Canadian
manufacturer DDGM as the contractor for this order.
The AVGP comes in three variants: the **Cougar**, the
**Grizzly** and the **Husky**. The Canadian Forces order
later led to a major contract with the US Marine Corps
(USMC) for the 8 x 8 version of the Piranha, and later
to an even larger vehicle procurement by the US
Army TACOM (Tank Automotive and Armaments
Command) for the National Guard of Saudi Arabia.

GKN teamed up with MOWAG in 1990 to produce
the Piranha family of wheeled armoured vehicles to
meet a number of requirements in the UK's FFLAV
(Future Family of Light Armoured Vehicles).

The basic structure of the Piranha can protect its
occupants against small-arms fire and shell splinters,
whilst the layout of the vehicle is conventional for an
APC. The driver sits at the front with the engine to his
right, whilst the main armament is normally situated
in the centre of the vehicle and the troop compartment at the rear. The troops access the vehicle
through two outward-opening doors in the rear of the
vehicle, and there are firing ports in the side and rear
of the hull. All members of the Piranha family are
amphibious, powered by two propellers mounted at
the rear of the hull.

There are a vast number of different variants of
the Piranha in the different wheel combinations.
Some of the more common include the fitting of a
GIAT TS-90 90 mm turret, transforming the APC into
an AFV. Other common variants include recovery
vehicles and anti-tank models, equipped with HOT
ATGWs. Optional equipment on all models includes
night vision equipment, NBC protection and air-
conditioning systems.

*This version is known as the Kodiak in the Canadian Army*

*Piranha III H 8 x 8 APC of the Danish Army*

### SPECIFICATION:
**Crew:** 15
**Armament:** depends on model
**Ammunition:** depends on model
**Dimensions:** length 6.4 m; width 2.5 m; ground
clearance 0.5 m
**Weights:** empty 8,800 kg; loaded 12,300 kg
**Engine:** 6V-53T (diesel) developing 300 hp
**Performance:** road speed 100 km/h; range 780 km;
amphibious capability 10 km/h
**Armour:** 10 mm steel plate

# MRAV APC/AIFV

*The Multi Role Armoured Vehicle*

THE GOVERNMENTS OF THE UK AND GERMANY signed a contract in November 1999 for the collaborative development and initial production of the family of next generation armoured utility vehicles. The programme is known as the **Multi Role Armoured Vehicle (MRAV)** in the UK, and the **Gepanzertes Transport-Kraftfahrzeug (GTK)** in Germany. It is the first truly collaborative land-system project in Europe. The UK is participating in a collaborative programme with France and Germany for the development and initial production of a family of wheeled, armoured vehicles to meet the requirements of the three nations. The vehicle is essentially a German design, with Germany supplying the automotive components, the UK the basic chassis and GIAT Industries the mission module. Initially, the design will provide the APC and Command Vehicle versions but will also allow for the development of other variants using the same base vehicle.

Following a competition between two international consortia, an announcement was made on 22 April 1998, jointly with France and Germany, that Eurokonsortium (now known as ARTEC and consisting of Krauss-Maffei Wegmann and MaK, Alvis Vehicles and GIAT) had been selected as the preferred bidder. An extensive programme of work has been put in hand to negotiate satisfactory contract terms and conditions.

Two families of vehicle are required: one consisting of highly mobile, well-protected vehicles (known as M1P1s) designed to operate alongside the Challenger and the Warrior; and the other of less mobile, less well-protected vehicles (known as M2P2s) designed to work in areas where there is reduced direct fire threat. The MRAV replaces the utility CVR(T), Saxon GWR and FV430 family to meet a number of support functions. Around 1,400 medium mobility, medium protection vehicles will be required by the UK.

## SPECIFICATION:

**Crew:** 11
**Armament:** 12.7 mm machine-gun
**Dimensions:** length 7.9 m; height 2.4 m
**Weight:** 33,000 kg
**Engine:** 530 kW (ISO)
**Performance:** road speed 103 km/h; range 1,050 km
**Armour:** combination of steel and modular armour

# MT-LB APC

*MT-LB multi-purpose tracked vehicle*

THE **MT-LB** WAS DEVELOPED BY THE Soviet Union in the 1960s as the replacement for the older AT-P armoured artillery tractor. It was initially known in the West as the **M-1970** multi-purpose tracked vehicle until its true designation became known.

The MT-LB armoured tracked vehicle is fully amphibious, propelled in the water by its tracks. The low-silhouette MT-LB has a flat-track suspension consisting of six road wheels with no return rollers. The box-like welded steel plate hull has a crew compartment at the front, engine immediately behind on the left side, and a troop compartment at the rear which has inward-facing folding canvas seats for ten infantrymen. The flat hull roof has two forward-opening troop exit hatches. The infantry enter and leave the vehicle by two rear doors that are provided with firing ports. The total of four firing ports also include one on each side of the vehicle. The small turret to the right of the commander's position mounts a single 7.62 mm machine-gun. Standard equipment on all vehicles includes an NBC protection system.

The MT-LB is a multi-purpose vehicle. When used as an ARC or command vehicle, it can carry ten personnel besides its two-man crew (driver and commander-gunner). It is also used as a prime mover for various types of artillery. In this case it can also carry the artillery crew (six to ten personnel). It is frequently used as the mover for the T-12 100 mm anti-tank gun. As a cargo and general transport vehicle, it has a cargo capacity of 2.0 metric tons (towed load 6.5 metric tons). It has an enormous range of variants, including versions equipped with 80 mm and 120 mm mortars and the SA-13 Gopher SAM system, whilst Iraq uses the MT-LB as a self-propelled 120 mm mortar system. The MT-LB is currently in service with Bulgaria, Czechoslovakia, Finland, Poland, Hungary, Iraq and the former states of both the Soviet Union and Yugoslavia.

## SPECIFICATION:

**Crew:** 2 + 10
**Armament:** 1 x 7.62 mm machine-gun
**Ammunition:** 2,500 rounds
**Dimensions:** length 6.5 m; width 2.9 m; height 1.9 m; ground clearance 0.4 m
**Weight:** empty 9.700 kg; combat 11,900 kg
**Engine:** V-8 diesel developing 290 hp
**Performance:** road speed 70 km/h; range 500 km
**Armour:** 7–14 mm armour

# FRANCE
# Panhard Sagaie Light Tank/Recce Vehicle

*Panhard ERC 90 F4 Sagaie*

IN 1970, WHEN THE FRENCH ARMY ISSUED a requirement for a VAB (*Véhicule de l'Avant Blindé*), Panhard and Renault presented two prototypes each, with 4 x 4 and 6 x 6 configurations, all completely amphibious. Renault won the contract, and since then large numbers of the 4 x 4 and 6 x 6 VAB have been built. Taking advantage of the experience gained in this competition, Panhard began to develop its own range of 6 x 6 vehicles, including both reconnaissance vehicles and APCs. The first of the ERCs (*Engin de Reconnaissance Canon*) appeared in 1977 and was evaluated by the French Army between 1978 and 1980. It was decided to accept the **ERC 90 F4 Sagaie** into service, primarily with the French Rapid Deployment Force. The Sagaie has also been acquired by other countries, including Argentina, Niger and Mexico.

The all-welded hull provides the crew with protection from small-arms fire and shell splinters, whilst the hull floor has been specially adapted to provide additional protection against mines. The driver is seated at the front, the turret is in the centre and the engine and transmission are at the rear. All the vehicles within the range are powered by a militarised version of the Peugeot V-6 petrol engine, developing 155 hp at 5,250 rpm. One interesting feature about the vehicle is that the central pair of wheels can be raised off the ground for road travel. The basic model can ford to a depth of 1.2 m without preparation, although two different amphibious versions of the Sagaie have already been developed.

The turret fitted to the Sagaie is the GIAT TS-90. This is armed with a 90 mm gun firing a range of ammunition, including canister, HE, HEAT and APFSDS, 20 rounds being carried in the turret. In addition to this a 7.62 mm machine-gun is mounted coaxially, with another on the turret roof for air defence, and 2,000 rounds of ammunition are carried.

Different options for the vehicle include a wheeled amphibious version, an amphibious version powered by hydrojets, an NBC system, air-conditioning system/heater and additional storage for ammunition. A land navigation system can also be fitted, essential for when the vehicle is used in the desert.

## SPECIFICATION:

**Crew:** 3
**Armament:** 90 mm F1 rifled gun, 7.62 mm coaxial machine-gun, 7.62 mm optional anti-aircraft machine-gun
**Ammunition:** 20 rounds, 90 mm; 2,000 rounds coaxial and anti-aircraft
**Dimensions:** length 7.693 m; height 2.254 m; width 2.495 m; road ground clearance 0.294 m; cross-country 0.344 m
**Weight:** loaded 8,300 kg
**Engine:** Peugeot V-6 petrol; output 155 hp
**Performance:** range 700 km; road speed 95 km/h; max. water speed 7.2 km/h

# FRANCE
# Panhard VBL Light Tank/Recce Vehicle

*Panhard VBL with MILAN ATGW*

*Panhard VBL scout vehicle*

IN 1978 THE FRENCH ARMY ISSUED A requirement for a vehicle weighing less than 3,500 kg to fulfil two basic roles. Firstly, it was to provide the basis of the French anti-tank defence, and secondly it was to provide a vehicle for the reconnaissance/scout role. After an open competition, designs from Renault and Panhard were accepted and they were commissioned to provide trials vehicles for what was to be known as the **VBL** (*Véhicule Blindé Léger*). Following trials from 1983 to 1985, the Panhard was accepted into service with the French Army. Although no initial order was forthcoming due to spending cuts, the French Government has since ordered over 3,600. There has also been a strong marketing drive for the product, with both Portugal and Mexico taking delivery of orders, as well as a number of African countries.

The hull of the Panhard VBL is of all-welded steel, varying in thickness from 5 to 11 mm. This offers the crew adequate protection from small-arms fire and shell splinters. In order to reduce costs the engine is the same as on the Peugeot 505 and 605 cars – the Peugeot XD 3T, a 4-cylinder turbo-charged diesel engine producing 95 hp. This also allows the VBL to have a maximum road speed of 95 km/h, greatly increasing its versatility on the battlefield. The layout is conventional, with the engine at the front and the crew compartment at the rear. The driver sits on the left of the compartment with the commander on the right, both crew members being protected by bullet-proof windows 33.5 mm–49 mm thick. The VBL is equipped with Michelin combat tyres, allowing it to travel over 50 km with punctures, and it is readily amphibious, convertible after only two minutes' of preparation. It is propelled in the water by a single propeller mounted beneath the rear of the hull.

The combat version of the VBL has a crew of three and is armed with the MILAN anti-tank system, along with six missiles, as well as a 7.62 mm machine-gun and 3,000 rounds of ammunition. The reconnaissance version only has a crew of two, the driver and the commander/radio operator, while its armament consists of a 7.62 mm or 12.7 mm machine-gun. In addition to these two basic models there are plans for a wide variety of variants for export, including command vehicles, internal security vehicles and anti-aircraft vehicles.

## SPECIFICATION:

**Crew:** 2 for intelligence or 3 for combat
**Armament:** combat 7.62 mm machine-gun and MILAN, plus 3 x 5.56 mm FAMAS rifles and 9 hand grenades; intelligence version, 7.62 mm machine-gun, or 12.7 mm M2 HB machine-guns; 2 x 5.56 mm FAMAS rifles + 6 hand grenades. Optional, LRAC anti-tank launcher + 12 rockets
**Ammunition:** 3,000 rounds/6 missiles; 3,000 rounds/or 1,200
**Dimensions:** length 3.7 m; height to hull top 1.7 m, 2.14 m with machine-gun; width 2.02 m; ground clearance 0.37 m
**Weight:** 3,590 kg with NBC system, 3,550 kg without; loaded weight 2,890 kg; empty weight 2,850 kg
**Engine:** Peugeot 4-cylinder turbo-charged diesel; output 105 hp
**Performance:** range 600 km; road speed 95 km/h; water speed 4.5 km/h
**Armour:** 5–11.5 mm steel

## GERMANY
# Panzerhaubitze 2000 SP Artillery

*Krauss-Maffei Wegmann Panzerhaubitze 2000*

IN 1986 ITALY, THE UNITED KINGDOM and Germany agreed to terminate the trilateral co-operation on the PzH 155-1 (SP 70) programme, and German industry was asked to submit bid proposals for the PzH 155 mm (front-driven). The **PzH 2000** 155 mm self-propelled howitzer was developed by Krauss-Maffei Wegmann and Co. GmbH for the German Army. Wegmann received a contract in March 1996 for the production of 185 units, with deliveries between 1998 and 2002, for use in the 'crisis reaction forces' as well as for first deployment in the Main Forces.

The German PzH 2000 (Panzerhaubitze 2000) is Germany's next-generation 155 mm self-propelled howitzer, and is among the most capable howitzers in the world. The required range of 30 km with standard NATO ammunition, or almost 40 km with assisted ammunition, is achieved by the newly developed 52 calibre 155 mm armament, and also by the new Modular Charge System Propelling. Continued use of the in-service bag charges is also possible. The 155 mm armament is automatically laid at high speed and precision, its position is checked after every fired round and, if necessary, it is relayed automatically. The automatic shell loading system includes different semi-automatic and manual back-up modes, an automatic primer magazine, and automatic inductive fuse setting. A hybrid GPS navigation system is used for navigating and determining the position of the gun barrel. An on-board ballistic computer with a radio data link to an external fire-control command post enables the gun to conduct fire missions quickly and independently from any unprepared firing position after receiving target position and ammunition data. The PzH 2000 is also able to automatically lay its main armament in accordance with laying and ammunition data radio-transmitted by a fire-control command post.

Following completion of engineering trials and operation tests including low and high-temperature tests in Shilo, Canada, and Yuma, USA, life crew clearance was awarded by BWB in March 1994, with the user declaration of deployment readiness being approved in November 1995. Approval for introduction into service was given by the German armed forces in January 1996. Series production began immediately, with a projected release date of 1998. The 185 units under production will be delivered between 1998 and 2002. Four PzH 2000 prototypes have been under intensive testing since August 1993. As well as the clearance given by the BWB and the cold and hot-weather trials, logistic troop trials were successfully performed. Tests performed by the Swedish Coast Artillery in May 1996 proved the accuracy of the PzH 2000 against moving sea targets. The system achieved a high accuracy against a towed sea target (4x4 m) at a range of between 6,000 and 8,000 m. A constant pattern was shown in the points of impact that changed exactly in accordance with the moving target. Only four rounds would be needed to destroy the target. The success of these trials was confirmed by participating artillery and coast artillery inspectors from Norway, Finland, Sweden and Denmark, as well as military onlookers from Italy, the Netherlands and Germany.

### SPECIFICATION:

**Crew:** 5
**Armament:** 155 mm L52 howitzer, 7.62 mm MG3 machine-gun
**Ammunition:** 60 x 155 mm projectiles; 288 modular charge modules
**Dimensions:** length 11.669 m; height 3.46 m; width 3.58 m; ground clearance 0.44 m
**Weight:** loaded 55,330 kg; ground pressure 0.98 kg/cm$^2$
**Engine:** MTU 881 diesel; output 1,000 hp
**Performance:** range 420 km; road speed 60 km/h
**Armour:** n/a

# Piranha Light Tank/Recce Vehicle

*The Piranha Light Tank (MOWAG Motorwagenfabrik AG)*

THE SWISS FIRM MOWAG originally developed the **Piranha** range of armoured cars and personnel carriers in the 1960s. They are a private venture and their designs have been operated by the Swiss and Canadian armed forces in particular, as well as the US Marine Corps, though they have also seen service in the armies of Chile, Ghana, Liberia, Nigeria and Sierra Leone. The development of the **Piranha Light Tank/Recce Vehicle** started in 1992 and was completed in 1994 as an improvement on the already existing MOWAG Piranha (8 x 8). The new 10 x 10 version gives an increased payload capability, an enlargement in internal volume and an increased ballistic protection.

The all-welded steel hull of the original Piranha provided protection against 7.62 mm small-arms fire, and the new version has additional protection against 14.5 mm small-arms fire over the frontal arc. The layout of the vehicle is similar to existing models within the Piranha family. The driver is situated to the left, with the power-pack to his right, and the turret in the centre. The rear compartment can contain up to 38 rounds of 105 mm ammunition, as well as the fuel tank and winch.

The standard engine is a Detroit developing 350 hp, though this can potentially be upgraded to an MTU Diesel developing 400 hp. The steering is power-assisted on the four front road wheels. The three rear axles are permanently driven and the two front ones can be engaged as and when is deemed necessary. All members of the Piranha family are amphibious, being driven by two propellers at the rear of the hull.

The turret is equipped with a GIAT 105 mm rifled gun capable of firing standard NATO ammunition, including the APFDS. A 7.26 mm machine-gun is mounted coaxially with the main armament. In addition to this there is a grenade-launching machine fitted as standard.

There are a number of variants of the Piranha, including versions with air defence turrets, Bofors 40 mm L/70 turrets and the Oerlikon Aerospace ADATS missile system.

## SPECIFICATION:

**Crew:** 4
**Armament:** 105 mm main gun, 7.62 mm coaxial machine-gun
**Ammunition:** 38 rounds; 2,000 rounds, coaxial
**Dimensions:** length 8.75 m; height 2.99 m; width 2.60 m; ground clearance 0.57 m
**Weight:** loaded 18,000 kg
**Engine:** Detroit Diesel; output 350 hp
**Performance:** range 800 km; road speed 100 km/h
**Armour:** n/a

# PT-76/85 Light Tank/Recce Vehicle

THE **PT-76** LIGHT AMPHIBIOUS TANK was developed shortly after the end of World War II, primarily for an amphibious reconnaissance role, and was accepted for service in 1950. Total production is believed to have been over 7,000 vehicles, with the last entering service in 1967. Many of its automotive and sub-components are also used in the BTR-50, SA-6 Gainful SAM system and ZSU-23-4.

The hull is of welded construction. The driver is seated in the front centre of the hull and has a one-piece hatch cover that swings open to the right. Three periscopes are mounted forward of the hatch, and the centre one can be raised to allow the driver to see over the trim vane when swimming, or can be replaced with a TVN-28 IR periscope with a 60 m range.

The engine is in the rear, being the same engine that is used in one bank of that fitted to the T-55 MBT. The PT-76 is fully amphibious, being propelled in the water by two water jets mounted at the rear of the hull. To increase the operational range the vehicle can be fitted with additional fuel tanks, which can be either drums or the flat type mounted on the T-55.

The two-man turret is welded steel, with the loader on the right side and the commander, who also serves as gunner, on the left. The turret has a single large, oval-shaped hatch cover that opens forwards. On the left side of the hatch is a cupola for the tank commander that has three vision blocks and can be rotated 360° by hand. The commander has a 4X optical sight mounted to the left of the main armament. The loader has a periscope mounted on the turret roof forward of the hatch.

The main armament is the 76.2 mm D-56T gun which was also used on the T-34/76 tanks during World War II. The gun has a maximum rate of fire of 6 to 8 rpm and a maximum range of 13,290 m in indirect fire mode. A 7.62 mm SGMT machine-gun is

*A PT-76 drives ashore after an amphibious landing*

mounted to the right of the main armament, and many PT-76s have been fitted with a 12.7 mm DShKM anti-aircraft machine-gun.

The PT-76's main drawbacks are its large size, lack of NBC and night-fighting equipment, and very thin armour that can be penetrated by a .50 calibre machine-gun. Because of this the PT-76 has been replaced in the former Soviet units by more modern equipment, but it is still in service with many Third World nations. China has also produced a more powerful variant, and an Israeli company, NIMDA, has also upgraded the basic PT-76.

## SPECIFICATIONS:

**Crew:** 3
**Armament:** 76.2 mm rifled D-56TS gun, 7.62 mm SGMT coaxial machine-gun, 12.7 mm DShKM machine-gun (optional anti-aircraft gun)
**Ammunition:** 40 rounds, main gun; 1,000 rounds, machine-gun
**Dimensions:** length 7.625 m; height 2.255 m; width 3.14 m; ground clearance 0.37 m
**Weight:** loaded 14,600 kg; ground pressure 0.50 kg/cm²
**Engine:** V6B 6-cylinder diesel; output 240 hp
**Performance:** range 370 km (to 480 with auxiliary tanks); road speed 44 km/h; water speed 8–9 km/h
**Armour:** 11–14 mm front; 11–17 mm turret; 8 mm turret top

SOUTH AFRICA
# Ratel APC/AIFV

THE ORIGINAL WHEELED VEHICLE OF CHOICE with the South African Army was the Alvis Saracen 6 x 6 APC, of which 250 were supplied by the British in the 1950s. When the South Africans decided to manufacture their own APCs and AIFVs they initially built a variation of the French Panhard AML known as the Eland, constructed under licence by Sandock-Austral. From 1968 onwards this same company was commissioned to create a totally new vehicle that would fulfil the roles assigned to it by the South African Infantry and Armoured Corps. The first prototypes were delivered in 1974, and the **Ratel** entered production, with the first vehicles being completed just two years later in 1978. The **Mark I** was superseded by the **Mark 2**, and the final production models of the Ratel were delivered in 1989, with another 1,000 having been produced for the home and export markets.

The basic model is the **Ratel 20** IFV, which can carry a crew of 11 – commander, gunner, driver, anti-aircraft gunner and seven fully equipped infantrymen. The hull is all-welded and offers protection against 7.62 mm small-arms fire and shell splinters, whilst additional armour over the frontal arc offers protection against 12.7 mm armour-piercing rounds. The driver is positioned at the front of the vehicle, and behind him is located the two-man all-welded turret, which is equipped with a 20 mm dual-feed cannon and a coaxial 7.62 mm machine-gun. A similar weapon is mounted at the rear of the vehicle for anti-aircraft purposes. The crew compartment is situated at the rear of the vehicle, with a door at the rear. The Ratel is powered by a Model D 3256 BTFX 6-cylinder turbo-

*Ratel fire support vehicle with 90 mm gun and roof-mounted 7.62 mm machine-gun*

charged diesel developing 282 hp, which allows for a top road speed of 105 km/h.

There are a large number of variants of the Ratel, including a version equipped with a 90 mm main armament which acts as a fire support vehicle. The main armament can fire either HEAT or HE rounds, and around 69 rounds are carried. Other notable variants include a late-production model that mounts an 81 mm mortar. The Ratel has excelled on operations with the South Africans in Angola, and it has also seen service with Moroccan forces.

### SPECIFICATION:
**Crew:** 11
**Armament:** 1 x 20 mm main gun, 1 x 7.62 mm coaxial machine-gun, 2 x 7.62 mm anti-aircraft machine-gun
**Ammunition:** 1,200 rounds, 20 mm; 6,000 rounds, 7.62 mm
**Dimensions:** length 7.2 m; width 2.5 m; height 2.9 m
**Weight:** empty 16,500 kg; combat 18,500 kg
**Engine:** D 3256 BTFX 6-cylinder turbo-charged diesel developing 282 hp
**Performance:** road speed 105 km/h; range 1,000 km; fording capacity 1.2 m
**Armour:** 20 mm front; 10 mm at sides and rear

# Roland SP Artillery

*The Roland SAM system of the German Army is based on the Marder 1 chassis*

STARTING ITS DEVELOPMENT FROM the early 1960s, the **Roland** short-range air defence missile system is currently produced by Euromissile, based in Fontenay-aux-Roses, France. Euromissile is a consortium set up by Aérospatiale-Matra of France and Daimler Chrysler Aerospace of Germany (now merged to form the EADS company with CASA of Spain). The Roland entered service with the French Army in 1977, and is in service with ten countries, including France and Germany.

The Roland system is effective against air threats from extremely low to medium altitude. It is available as a stand-alone weapon system on a single vehicle or, since 1995, as an air-portable shelter, **Roland**

**Carol**. Twenty of these systems have been delivered to the French Army, and eleven to the German Air Force. French Army tracked systems are mounted on vehicles based on the AMX-30 main battle tank, while German Army systems are installed on Marder tracked vehicles. In both cases, two missiles are held in a ready-to-launch position, whilst an additional eight missiles are carried in two automatic loaders in the body of the vehicle. Over 650 of these two systems have been produced.

The two-stage missile solid propellant missile is 2.4 m long with a span of 50 m and a diameter of 16 cm. It has a range of 16 km and an average cruising speed of Mach 1.6. To date the Roland is in

*A French Army Roland system fires a SAM missile*

*The French Army Roland SAM system is based on the chassis of the AMX-30 MBT*

service with a number of countries other than France, including Argentina, Brazil, Iraq, Spain, the USA and Venezuela.

As part of contracts with OCCAR, the European Defence Procurement Agency, and the French Army, a programme to upgrade the Roland missile system is in progress. The modernisation includes a new command and control system and the fitting of the infra-red Glaive sight from SAGEM for automatic multi-channel target tracking. The first prototype fire unit was completed in June 1999, and trials began in September 1999. The upgraded Roland will be called **Roland M3S**. The second prototype in the CAROL shelter-based configuration was completed in October 1999. (CAROL is a static, shelter-based version of the Roland SAM system – one was used by the Argentinians to defend Stanley airport during the Falklands War.)

## SPECIFICATION:

**Range:** maximum 6,000 m; minimum 700–2,000 m
**Altitude:** 5,500 m
**Basic load on vehicle:** 10 missiles
**Detection range:** 16.5 km
**Reaction time:** 4–10 sec
**Firing time:** 1st shooting: 8–10 sec, later shooting: 2–6 sec
**Speed:** Mach 1.6
**Reload time:** approximately 10 sec
**Probability of hit:** 80 per cent
**Warhead:** HE hollow charge
**Chassis:** AMX-30, Marder APC, trucks, or in fixed shelters

# Rooikat Light Tank/Recce Vehicle

*Rooikat reconnaissance vehicle*

**D**EVELOPMENT OF THE **ROOIKAT Light Tank/ Recce Vehicle** started in 1976, and it was unveiled in 1988 as an 8 x 8 vehicle equipped with a 76 mm gun. The chassis of the vehicle was constructed by Sandock-Austral, manufacturers of other South African AFVs and APCs such as the Eland and the Ratel. The turret was designed, developed, manufactured and supported by LEW. The turret sports a proprietary 62 calibre-length high-pressure 76 mm GT-4 tank gun, firing a range of HE, PRAC (Practice) and APFSDS ammunition.

The Rooikat is an all-welded steel construction with frontal armour proof against 23 mm AP (Armour Piercing). The driver is positioned at the front, the turret in the centre and the engine at the rear. The power-pack of the vehicle consists of a V-10 cylinder water-cooled diesel develo-ping 563 hp. Standard equipment on this model also includes vehicle intercom, radios and a chemical and biological overpressure collective system.

The **Rooikat LMT-105** is a development of the Rooikat 76 mm currently in series production by LEW for the South African National Defence Force, and is the turret fitted to the **Rooikat 105 mm** export model. This version is equipped with the LEW 52 calibre-length full-pressure 105 mm GT-7 tank gun, exhibiting low peak firing forces due to the utilisation of an advanced hydropneumatic recoil system. This gun has been subjected to a stringent qualification regime and fires the full range of NATO 105 mm ammunition, including APFSDS. In its advanced configuration (with stabilised panoramic commander sight and stabilised gunner sight incorporating thermal imager), the LMT-105 turret boasts formidable hunter-killer, day/night and fire-on-the-move capabilities derived from fire and gun control technologies developed for main battle tank turrets.

The vehicle is equipped with two banks of 81 mm smoke grenade launchers, mounted in a forward firing position on each side of the turret. The system is electrically operated. The smoke grenades form a dense protective smoke screen, which can be sustained using an exhaust smoke generator.

The Rooikat can withstand the blast of a TM46 anti-tank mine and provide full protection to the four-man crew. Ballistic protection against 24 mm ammunition is provided over the frontal arc. The Rooikat's eight-wheel configuration allows the vehicle to maintain mobility even after the loss of any wheel, caused for example by a land mine detonation. Also, the vehicle is equipped with run-flat inserts which allow mobility after the loss of pressure in all eight wheels. Collective overpressure and air filter systems protect the crew against chemical and biological attack. An automatic fire explosion suppression system is also available.

---

## SPECIFICATION:

**Crew:** 4
**Armament:** GT-4 76 mm 62-calibre high-pressure tank gun, 1 x 7.62 mm coaxial machine-gun, 1 x 7.62 mm anti-aircraft machine-gun
**Ammunition:** 48 rounds, 76 mm; 3,600 rounds, 7.62 mm
**Dimensions:** length 8.2 m; width 2.9 m; height 2.8 m
**Weight:** combat 28,000 kg
**Engine:** V-10 water-cooled diesel developing 563 hp
**Performance:** road speed 120 km/h; range 1,000 km; fording capability 1.5 m
**Armour:** proof against 23 mm AP

# SA-8 Gecko SP Artillery

*SA-8 Gecko low-altitude SAM system*

THE **SA-8 GECKO** IS A SINGLE-STAGE, solid-fuel, short-range, low-altitude, all-weather SAM system. The first production version of this system was identified as **SA-8a**, which only had four launcher rails and exposed missiles. The **SA-8b** typically has two BAZ-5937 resupply/transloader vehicles, carrying 18 missiles each, boxed in sets of three. This system is also air transportable.

The SA-8a high-acceleration missile has a launch weight of about 130 kg. Maximum speed is Mach 2.4, minimum altitude is 25 m, and maximum effective altitude 5,000 m. The minimum range is 1,500 m and the maximum range 12,000 m. The SA-8b, introduced in 1980, is mounted in a rectangular launch box and incorporates improved guidance and higher speed, providing an increased maximum range of 15,000 m. The warhead of both missiles is fitted with proximity and contact fuses, and the 19 kg warhead's lethal radius at low altitude is about 5 m. The system reload time is five minutes.

The SA-8 transporter erector launcher and radar vehicle is a six-wheeled design designated BAZ-5937. Four command-guided missiles are carried ready to launch, two on either side. The driver's compartment at the front of the vehicle has accommodation for two, the driver and commander, with access via a hatch in the roof. The engine is at the very rear, and the vehicle is fully amphibious, being propelled in the water by two water jets at the rear of the hull. The vehicle is fitted with an air filtration and overpressure NBC system, together with infra-red systems for the commander and driver.

There are at least three major families of SA-8 launch vehicles. The first, a pre-series prototype, had a very blunt nose. The standard production model has a sharper nose, and there are variants of this vehicle that feature minor changes in the detail of hull fittings. The SA-8b vehicle is basically similar to the SA-8a vehicle, aside from the launcher that accommodates six missile canisters.

Each battery has two missile transloaders based on the same chassis, with a long tarpaulin-covered structure covering the cargo space and crane which slides to the rear when operating.

## SPECIFICATION:

**Crew:** 3
**Armament:** SA-8
**Ammunition:** 6 missiles
**Chassis/Carriage:** BAZ-5937
**Dimensions:** length 9.1 m; width 2.8 m; height 4.2 m
**Weight:** 9,000 kg
**Engine:** D20K300 diesel
**Performance:** road speed 80 km/h; range 500 km

# Saxon APC/AIFV

THE **SAXON ARMOURED PERSONNEL CARRIER**, originally known by the designation **AT105**, was first put into production in 1976 in order to replace the earlier AT100 and AT104, which had sold in small numbers on the export market. The AT105 was a completely new design using many components from the Bedford Mk 4 x 4 four-tonne truck, already a standard vehicle in the British Army. In 1983 the British Ministry of Defence placed its first orders for the Saxon, and the British Army continued to order the vehicle until 1990, when they had ordered a total of 524 vehicles. Post 1990 an export model of the Saxon appeared on the market, equipped with an improved Cummins 6BT 5.91 litre turbo-charged six-cylinder diesel engine developing 160 hp, which was coupled to a fully automatic transmission.

The basic model of the AT105 Saxon has an all-welded steel hull that offers complete protection against small-arms fire (including 7.62 mm AP rounds at point-blank range), as well as HE shells bursting at least 10 m from the vehicle. The driver sits at the front of the vehicle, with the engine to his right or left depending on whether it is a right- or left-hand-drive vehicle.

The troop compartment is at the rear of the hull, with the personnel sitting four to each side of the compartment. There are twin doors at the very rear of the vehicle and a door on each side for ease of access. There are also firing points and vision blocks in the doors, with additional firing ports along both sides of the hull. The commander's cupola in the roof is fixed, and a 7.62 mm machine-gun can be pintle

*Saxon APC in service with the British Army in Bosnia*

mounted if required. In recent years this has often been replaced with a one-man turret with a 7.62 mm machine-gun for better protection.

There are numerous variants of the Saxon available on the market. The most popular in use in the British Army include the Saxon Recovery Vehicle, equipped with a Hudson Wharton capstan 5,000 kg armoured winch. This device can handle vehicles weighing up to 16,000 kg, and is generally operated by the Royal Electrical and Mechanical Engineers. Other popular variants include those modified for internal security purposes, which are often armed with five-shot 37 mm riot guns.

---

## SPECIFICATION:

**Standard British Army model**

**Crew:** 2 + 8–10

**Dimensions:** length 5.169 m; height with turret top 2.86 m; width 2.489 m; ground clearance 0.29 m

**Weight:** empty 9,940 kg; loaded 11,660 kg

**Engine:** Bedford 6-cylinder diesel, output 164 hp

**Performance:** range 480 km; road speed 96 km/h; fording capability 1.12 m

**Armour:** proof against 7.62 mm/0.30 AP rounds at point-blank range

AUSTRIA

# Steyr-Daimler-Puch Pandur APC/AIFV

THE **PANDUR** 6 X 6 FAMILY OF WHEELED armoured vehicles has been developed by Steyr-Daimler-Puch of Austria. It has been operational with the Austrian Army since 1996 and is in production for the Kuwait National Guard and the Belgian Army. Slovenia has ordered 70 vehicles to be built under licence. The US Army has awarded a contract for up to 50 Pandur vehicles to form the basis of the Armoured Ground Mobility System.

For the reconnaissance and fire support role the vehicle is equipped with a Cockerill 90 mm LCTS turret with a Mark 8 gun, coaxial 7.62 mm machine-gun and 7.62 mm cupola machine-gun. Four smoke grenade launchers are fitted on either side of the turret.

The armoured personnel carrier is armed with a 12.7 mm machine-gun and a 7.62 mm general-purpose machine-gun. Six smoke grenade launchers are fitted on either side of the turret. A long-bodied variant accommodates the driver and commander and ten fully equipped troops.

Armour protection against 12.7 mm weapon systems is provided in the frontal 30-degree arc and against 7.62 mm calibre ammunition all round. A spall liner and mine protection carpet are installed to minimise the secondary effects of armour penetration and mines. The drive train and steering linkages are protected within the armoured hull.

Design features to reduce the thermal signature of the vehicle include a thermally insulated exhaust system and the use of infra-red absorbing paint. The design of vehicle surfaces has been computer optimised to minimise the radar cross-section of the vehicle. The noise signature has been reduced with engine and exhaust silencing systems.

*A Pandur operating with KFOR in Kosovo in 2000 (VS-Books Carl Schulze)*

The Pandur vehicle is powered by a Steyr WD 612.95 diesel engine, rated at 195 kW (260 hp). The hydraulically controlled automatic Allison transmission has torque converter and lockup clutch. The vehicle's computer system gives electronic control of systems such as gear locks and clutches, and the maintenance and repair diagnostic system, with visual and acoustic warnings. The two steered axles allow manoeuvrability after damage to the first axle. A tyre inflation system gives optimised traction on all terrain due to continuously adjustable tyre pressure.

### SPECIFICATION:
**Austrian Army APC**
**Crew:** 2 + 8
**Armament:** 1 x 12.7 mm machine-gun, 1 x 7.62 mm machine-gun, 2 x 3 smoke grenade launchers
**Ammunition:** 1,000 rounds, 12.7 mm
**Dimensions:** length 5.7 m; width 2.5 m; height 1.8 m
**Weight:** empty 9,800 kg; combat 13,000 kg
**Engine:** Steyr WD 612.95 6-cylinder turbo-charged diesel developing 260 hp
**Performance:** road speed 100 km/h; range 650 km; fording capability 1.2 m
**Armour:** 8 mm steel

96

# Stingray Light Tank/Recce Vehicle

*Cadillac Gage Stingray 1 light tanks of the Royal Thai Army*

OUTSIDE THE TRADITIONAL MBT MARKET there exists a range of countries whose needs are somewhat different. Whether because of expense or infrastructure, they are unwilling to invest in the complicated MBTs of today's market, preferring lighter tanks with greater simplicity and flexibility. The **Stingray** was developed to fulfil this market by Cadillac Gage in the early 1980s. By 1984 there was a working prototype of the vehicle, and in 1986 it was sent for trials in Thailand. This resulted in an order for 108 Stingray tanks for the Royal Thai Army being placed in 1987, and the order was fulfilled between 1988 and 1990.

The turret and the hull of the vehicle are of an all-welded construction, which offers complete protection against small-arms fire and shell splinters, whilst additional appliqué or ERA armour can be added to the vehicle to provide extra protection against HEAT and equivalent projectiles. The main armament of the vehicle is the British-made Royal Ordnance L7 105 mm, which can fire all types of NATO ammunition, including APFSDS. There is also a 7.62 mm machine-gun fitted coaxially, and either a 7.62 mm or a 12.7 mm machine-gun fitted onto the roof for air defence. Thirty-two rounds of main gun ammunition are carried, along with 2,200 rounds of 7.62 mm.

The power-plant of the vehicle is the Detroit Diesel Allison 8V-92TA which is capable of developing 535 hp and provides a maximum road speed of 70 km/h over a range of 500 km. The suspension used is that successfully developed for the M109 self-propelled howitzer. There is a second generation of Stingray tanks currently at the prototype stage, incorporating improved armour and gun recoil systems. To date there are no orders for this model.

---

## SPECIFICATION:

**Crew:** 4

**Armament:** L7 LRF 105 mm main gun, 1 x 7.62 mm coaxial machine-gun, 1 x 12.7 mm anti-aircraft machine-gun

**Ammunition:** 32 rounds, 105 mm; 2,400 rounds, 7.62 mm; 1,100 rounds, 12.7 mm

**Dimensions:** length 9.3 m; width 2.7 m; height 2.5 m

**Weight:** empty 17,237 kg; combat 19,051 kg

**Engine:** Detroit Diesel Allison 8V-92TA 535 hp liquid-cooled turbo-charged 2-stroke V-8 diesel engine; Allison XTG-411-2A automatic transmission

**Performance:** road speed 70 km/h; range 500 km; fording capability 1.2 m

**Armour:** Cadoly steel; turret armour is reported to defeat 14.5 mm rounds over frontal arc and 7.62 mm rounds from any angle

# T-72 MBT

*T-72M4 CZ MBT undergoing snorkelling trials*

THE **T-72 URAL** IS ONE OF THE MOST successful of all Russian MBTs and has been sold to a remarkable number of friendly states. This was the tank that 'threatened' the West in the final years of Communist rule, and it was the mainstay of the Soviet and Warsaw Pact armies. Today there are still over 18,000 in service with Algeria, Angola, Armenia, Azerbaijan, Belarus, Bulgaria, Croatia, Czech Republic*, Finland, Georgia, Hungary, India*, Iran, Iraq, Kazakhstan, Kyrgystan, Libya, Poland*, Romania, Russia, Sierra Leone, Slovakia*, Syria, Tadjikistan, Turkmenistan, Ukraine, Uzbekistan and Yugoslavia*. (The asterisked countries have built the T-72 themselves under licence.)

It was only in the early 1990s as the information became available that the full story of the development of the T-72 became known: when it was first seen by the West in 1977 there was confusion, as the T-64 had been misidentified as the T-72, and suddenly Western observers could see a different tank with different running gear. Now we know what happened. The Russian tank design bureau (*konstruktorskoye biuro*, or KB, in Russian) had been moved to the Urals during World War II to keep it away from the advancing Germans. Headed by Aleksandr Morozov, it was fantastically successful,

and it would produce the T-34 and its postwar successors the T-44, T-54 and T-55. In the late 1950s Khrushchev let Morozov return to his post-invasion location in Kharkov in the Ukraine, while continuing to run the Urals design bureau to provide competition. The Morozov KB produced the T-64 design; the Urals-based Uralvagon KB the T-72. Initially Morozov's design was successful, but expense and mechanical problems with the autoloader and engine soon led to a rethink. The T-72 design (Obiekt 172 – code-named Ural to show where its design originated) was reinstated, and the first prototype appeared in 1968. Following trials it was refined and entered initial production in 1972. These first vehicles were tested in service, improvements were made and full production began in 1974. So when the West first saw it, the confusion was understandable. The T-64 – a more radical design – would go on to serve only with Soviet forces. The T-72 was the true successor of the T-34 and and T-54.

The T-72 has three crew (driver, commander and gunner) and an autoloader, so the commander handles the coaxial machine-gun and AA 12.7 mm machine-gun on the turret top. The autoloader for the 125 mm smooth-bore stabilised gun carries 24 two-part rounds, usually a mix of APDS, HE and HEAT; all

*A T-72 Russian main battle tank (Tim Ripley)*

are fin-stabilised. The autoloader is capable of eight rounds a minute, although its reliability has always been in doubt. Range is *c.* 4,000 m for the APDS and HEAT rounds, 5,000 m for HE. The welded steel hull and turret of the T-72 were designed to provide a particularly low silhouette, and laminate passive armour 'hardened' the frontal arc. The hull carried the usual Soviet jettisonable fuel tanks at the rear, an unditching beam, and dozer blades and mine-clearing devices could be fitted. The many versions of the T-72 have seen major improvements to the armour – including various forms of reactive armour (in Russian EDZ – *elementy dinamcheskoi zashchity*, dynamic protection elements) from a standard fit of 151 bricks to the 227 of the **T-72AV**. The Shtora electro-optical jammer was also designed to confuse ATGW.

There were a number of different T-72 models, and many changes to the basic vehicle over the large production run. There were also differences between the Soviet T-72s and those sold for export, which usually had inferior armour and NBC equipment (see T-72M/M1 below). Each of the main versions also had command vehicle variants (designated with a K – so **T-72K/T-72AK/T-72BK**, etc.) which carried an extra communications package. T-72 designations also changed when they were modified to carry reactive armour – thus the T-72AV is the **T-72A** with reactive armour; the **T-72S1** was an export version of the S with reactive armour. The main versions following the T-72 itself were as follows. The **T-72A** was a major improvement package, entering service in 1979 with increased armour, improved gun/searchlight/sights/rangefinder, etc., the addition of 12 smoke dischargers, an additional rear turret stowage box, better engine/suspension, etc. The **T-72B** saw the T-72 upgraded to T-80 standard with improved armour

protection (particularly against HEAT rounds) and the ability to fire the AT-11 'Svir' laser-guided tank munition (which means it must carry a laser designator). T-72Bs without this ability were designated **T-72B1**. An upgraded armour package to the T-72B produced the **T-72BM** (other changes included upgrading to the T-80's fire-control system and an improved engine). The **T-72M** was the T-72A built in Poland and Czechoslovakia, and the **T-72M1** is an upgrade package to T-72A standard and is also the designation used for exported Russian T-72As.

---

## SPECIFICATION:

**Crew:** 3

**Armament:** 125 mm 2A46 smooth-bore main gun, 7.62 mm PKT coaxial machine-gun; 12.7 mm NSV commander's machine-gun

**Ammunition:** ranges from 39 rounds in T-72 to 46 in T-72S (including ATGW missiles); 2,000 rounds, 7.62 mm; 300 rounds, 12.7 mm

**Dimensions:** length of hull 6.95 m (gun forward 9.53 m); height 2.22 m; width (with skirts) 3.59 m; ground clearance 0.49 m

**Weight:** empty 38,600–42,000 kg; loaded 41,000–46,000 kg; ground pressure 0.72 kg/cm$^2$

**Engine:** V-12 piston air-cooled multi-fuel; output 780 hp–840 hp

**Performance:** 483 km range; 67 km/h road speed; 1.07 m fording capability

**Armour:** from 410 mm (T-72) to 950 mm (T-72BM) thick cast armour

# T-80 MBT

*T-80BV MBT with explosive reactive armour*

THE **T-80 MBT** WAS DESIGNED in an attempt to rationalise the Soviet tank fleet, which comprised both the T-64 and the T-72. The T-80 was intended to combine the best features of both vehicles. The original T-80 was introduced in 1979 and has been refined throughout various stages until the introduction of the **T-80UM** in the 1990s.

The basic development of the tank was undertaken at the Leningrad Kirov Plant, though production has since moved elsewhere. The T-80 retains the low silhouette of the earlier FSU tanks. The suspension consists of six forged steel-aluminium rubber-tyred road wheels, drive sprocket at the rear, idler at the front, and five return road wheels. The rubber-tyred road wheels are in two halves that are bolted together. The road wheel spacing is not identical and there are distinct gaps between the second and third, fourth and fifth, and fifth and sixth road wheels. The side skirt covers the return rollers. The rubber-bushed, double-pin track has rubber track pads and U-shaped track guides. The T-80 has a distinct oblong exhaust outlet in the hull rear. The

driver's hatch is centred at the top of a sharply sloped upper glacis. Integrated fuel cells and stowage containers give a streamlined appearance to the fenders. The tank has a toothed shovel/dozer blade on the front of the hull beneath the glacis. There are attachment points beneath the blade for the KMT-6 mine-clearing plough. The low, rounded turret is centred on the hull. The commander's cupola is on the right side of the turret; the gunner's hatch is on the left side. The 125 mm main gun has a four-section removable thermal shield. It has two sections in front of, and two sections to the rear of, the mid-tube bore evacuator. A 7.62 mm coaxial machine-gun is mounted to the right of the mantlet. The infra-red searchlight is mounted on the right of the main armament. Banks of electrically operated smoke dischargers are mounted on either side of the 125 mm gun/missile launcher, normally five on the left and four on the right.

The T-80 has a GTD-1000 gas-turbine engine developing 1,250 hp coupled to a manual transmission with five forward and one reverse gears. The

*T-80 MBT with supplementary fuel tanks on the rear hull*

glacis plate is of the laminate type for improved protection against kinetic energy and HEAT attack and there is a dozer blade under the nose of the vehicle. The turret is steel with an inner layer of special armour; the gunner sits on the left and the tank commander on the right. The T-80 MBT uses the same 125 mm gun and horizontal ammunition system as the T-72. The fire-control system is an improvement over that fitted to earlier former Soviet tanks. This tank can fire either the AT-8 Songster ATGM or four types of separate loading ammunition. These four rounds are HE-FRAG (FS), HEAT-FS, APFSDS-T and Flechette. A total of six AT-8 Songster ATGMs are carried, and these are identical to those launched by the T-64B MBT deployed some years ago. A 7.62 mm PKT machine-gun is mounted coaxially to the right of the main armament, and a 12.7 mm NSVT machine-gun is mounted on the commander's cupola. To extend the operational range of the T-80, additional fuel tanks can be mounted at the hull rear. These can be quickly jettisoned if required. Standard equipment includes snorkels for deep fording operations that are carried on the turret rear when not required, an overpressure-type NBC protection system, night vision equipment for all three crew members, an unditching beam carried across the hull rear and a laser warning device activated by laser rangefinders, laser designators or precision-guided munitions fitted

with a laser guidance device. Mounted on the turret rear is a large circular container that carries two snorkels. The larger one is the snorkel for the gas-turbine, with another one fitted onto the radiator grille by means of two adapters. This provides an air intake for the gas-turbine.

## SPECIFICATION:

**Crew:** 3
**Armament:** 125 mm 2A46 smooth-bore main gun, 7.62 mm coaxial PKT machine-gun, 12.7 mm NSVT commander's machine-gun, 8 x 81 mm smoke grenade dischargers
**Ammunition:** 39 rounds, main gun (28 in automatic loader); 1,250 rounds, coaxial; 450 rounds, anti-aircraft; 8 smoke grenades
**Dimensions:** length 9.656 m; height 2.202 m; width 3.589 m; ground clearance 0.446 m
**Weight:** loaded 46,000 kg; ground pressure 0.93 kg/cm²
**Engine:** gas turbine; output 1,250 hp
**Performance:** range 440 km; road speed 70 km/h; fording capability 1.2m, 6.0 m with preparation
**Armour:** n/a

# T-84 MBT

*The Ukraine's first venture into the tank industry, the T-84 (Tim Ripley)*

THE **T-84** IS THE FIRST VENTURE BY the independent Ukrainian arms industry into the main battle tank market. It was originally developed at the famed government-owned Kharkov Design Bureau before being produced at the Malyshev Factory. In 1993 the decision was taken to upgrade the Soviet-era T-80 in order to produce an MBT for both the home and export markets. The T-84 is essentially a T-80UD tank, a diesel-powered variant of the T-80, powered by an uprated 6TD-2 diesel engine. This engine develops 1,200 hp, giving the vehicle an improved power-to-weight ratio of about 27 hp/ton. The T-84 also includes the Shtora-1 electro-optical countermeasures system, the Arena vehicle protection system, improved tracks, thermal protection for the engine, and an air-conditioning system for the crew.

The 6TD-2 engine is situated at the rear and is less fuel thirsty than a turbine while generating 1,200 hp. There are currently plans to introduce a 1,500 hp version, along with a new transmission system consisting of seven forward and one reverse gears.

The armament consists of a Ukrainian-produced 125 mm KBA-3 main gun, fitted with an autoloader for 28 rounds. The fire-control system enables accurate fire in daylight for up to 5,000 metres for the AT-11 ATGM and up to 2,500 metres for main gun rounds. At night, the gunner's fire-control system gives a forward field of view of up to 1,200 metres, while the thermal imager extends this to 3,000 metres. It has been claimed that the main gun can fire as many as seven to nine rounds per minute, or two to three missiles, or four delayed detonation projectiles. As well as the main armament, a 7.62 mm machine-gun is mounted coaxially. There is also a 12.7 mm NSVT machine-gun mounted for the commander, which is primarily used in the anti-aircraft role.

In terms of protection, the turret of the T-84 is larger than that of the T-80 and is made from welded construction to give additional protection. The Shtora-1 vehicle-protection system is also fitted to this tank, in common with the T-90 and certain versions of the T-80. The Shtora-1 system works by sending out a series of intense infra-red pulses to disrupt the guidance systems of incoming missiles. It is reported to reduce the hit-probability of ATGMs with semi-automatic control systems (TOW, HOT, Dragon, and MILAN) up to five-fold, while missiles with laser-homing heads (Hellfire, Maverick and Copperhead) have a similarly reduced probability of hitting. It is also linked to an instant smoke screen system to provide additional protection for the tank. The Arena vehicle-protection system automatically detects incoming projectiles and launches a series of countermeasures to deal with them.

The T-84 can also be fitted with various types of mine-clearing equipment at the front of the hull, and there are two long-range fuel tanks and an unditching beam mounted at the rear.

## SPECIFICATION:

**Crew:** 3
**Armament:** 125 mm KBA-3 gun, 7.62 mm coaxial PKT machine-gun, 12.7 mm NSVT machine-gun, smoke grenade launchers
**Ammunition:** 45 rounds, main gun (28 in automatic loader); 1,250 rounds, coaxial; 450 rounds, anti-aircraft; 12 smoke grenades
**Dimensions:** length 9.664 m; height 2.215 m; width 3.775 m; ground clearance 0.515 m
**Weight:** loaded 46,000 kg; ground pressure 0.93 kg/cm$^2$
**Engine:** 6TD-2 twin-stroke, multi-fuel, fuel-injected; output 1,200 hp
**Performance:** range 560 km; road speed 60 km/h; fording capability 1.8 m, 5.0 m with preparation
**Armour:** n/a

# T-90 MBT

*T-90 Main Battle Tank (Jane's Information Group))*

THE **T-90** IS A COMPREHENSIVE UPGRADE of the T-72, incorporating a number of the features of the T-80, primarily as a stopgap before the rumoured introduction of an advance-technology MBT known as the T-95.

The T-90 retains the low silhouette of the earlier FSU tanks. The suspension consists of six large, die-cast, rubber-coated road wheels with the drive sprocket at the rear, idler at the front and three track-return rollers that support the inside of the track only. Shock absorbers are fitted at the first, second and sixth road wheel stations. There are side skirts that extend along the entire side of the tank. The front third of this skirt consists of armoured panels, whereas the rear two-thirds consist only of rubberised panels. There is an engine exhaust on the left side of the hull above the last road wheel. The glacis is well sloped, and is covered by second generation ERA bricks and a large transverse rib that extends horizontally across the glacis. The driver sits at the front of the hull and has a single-piece hatch cover that opens to the right, in front of which is a single wide-angle observation periscope. Integrated

fuel cells and stowage containers give a streamlined appearance to the fenders. The tank has a toothed shovel/dozer blade on the front of the hull beneath the glacis. There are attachment points beneath the blade for the KMT-6 mine-clearing plough. The low, rounded turret is centred on the hull. The commander's cupola is on the right side of the turret; the gunner's hatch is on the left side. The 125 mm main gun has a four-section removable thermal shield. It has two sections in front of, and two sections to the rear of, the mid-tube bore evacuator. A 7.62 mm coaxial machine-gun is mounted to the right of the mantlet. The T-90 mounts two infra-red searchlights on either side of the main armament; these are part of the Shtora ATGM defence system. The turret is covered with second-generation reactive armour on the frontal arc. There are additional ERA bricks on the turret roof to provide extra protection. There are banks of smoke mortars on either side of the turret. The T-90 is powered by the Model 84 V-84MS diesel engine, which produces 840 hp. This results in a power-to-weight ratio of only 18.06 hp/ton, which is considerably less than that of the T-80. The high level

of protection has been supplemented with the TShU-1-7 IR-jamming system, which is designed to disrupt the guidance of incoming ATGMs. This system consists of two infra-red lights, one on each side of the main gun, which continuously emit coded pulsed infra-red jamming when an incoming ATGM has been detected. The T-90 is also equipped with a laser warning package that warns the tank crew when it is a laser target. The T-90 retains the 125 mm 2A46-series main gun of the T-72 and T-80, and is capable of firing the AT-11 SNIPER laser-guided ATGM. The AT-11, which can penetrate 700 mm of RHAe (steel armour) out to 4,000 metres, gives the T-90 the ability to engage other MBTs, vehicle ATGMs, and even most helicopters before they can engage the T-90. The computerised fire-control system and laser rangefinder, coupled with the new gunner's thermal sight, permit the T-90 to engage targets while on the move and at night. Detailed information on the Agave gunner's thermal sight is not yet available, but this is probably a first-generation system and not as capable as current Western systems.

In many ways the T-90 is inferior to the T-80, particularly in terms of speed and power-to-weight ratio. However, the increased protection offered by ERA and the various electro-optical systems make it one of the best protected MBTs in the world.

*T-90 at speed*
*(Jane's Information Group))*

## SPECIFICATION:

**Crew:** 3
**Armament:** 125 mm smooth-bore 2A46M main gun, 7.62 mm PKT coaxial machine-gun, 12.7 mm NSVT anti-aircraft machine-gun, 8 x 81 mm smoke grenade launchers
**Ammunition:** 43 rounds, main gun; 2,000 rounds, coaxial; 300 rounds, anti-aircraft
**Dimensions:** length 9.53 m; height 2.226 m; width 3.78 m; ground clearance 0.47 m
**Weight:** loaded 46,500 kg; ground pressure 0.91 kg/cm$^2$
**Engine:** V-84MS 4-stroke 12-cylinder multi-fuel diesel; output 840 hp
**Performance:** range 550 km; road speed 60 km/h; fording capability 1.8m, 5.0m with preparation
**Armour:** n/a

# FRANCE
# VAB APC/AIFV

*GIAT Industries VAB with 20 mm gun turret*

THE FRENCH DECIDED IN THE LATE 1960s to equip their infantry battalions with both tracked and wheeled vehicles, and in 1970 they issued a set of specifications for a Forward Area Armoured Vehicle to meet a number of different roles for the infantry. In May 1974 Renault was chosen as the contractor for the job, and the first vehicles rolled off the production line in 1976. Since then the **VAB** has been selected for the armed forces of 15 countries: Argentina, Brunei, Central African Republic, Cyprus, France, Indonesia, Ivory Coast, Kuwait, Lebanon, Mauritius, Morocco, Norway, Oman, Qatar and the United Arab Emirates. The French Army has a fleet of almost 4,000 VAB vehicles.

The latest version of the VAB is the **VAB NG**, which is now ready to enter production. The vehicle can be fitted with a selection of weapon systems, including a 12.7 mm or 25 mm Dragar turret, an anti-tank missile launcher turret or a variety of mortar systems.

The VAB NG has a steel hull and bullet-proof glazing which provides all-round protection against 7.62 mm AP ammunition, and the front of the vehicle provides protection against armour-piercing rounds. A splinter-absorbent liner can be fitted in the crew compartment, and add-on armour with protection against 14.5 mm armour-piercing ammunition can be fitted on the sides. The 180-degree windscreen and side windows are bullet-proof, while the rear window is fitted with armoured shutters. An NBC protection system is integrated with the air-conditioning system.

The tactical mobility of the VAB is the result of a high torque turbo-diesel commercial engine, the Renault MIDS 06-20-45 (220 hp), a fully automatic gearbox, independent wheel suspension, large-size wheels, short wheel-base, on-the-move central tyre-inflation system and low ground pressure. The maximum road speed is 110 km/h. The VAB is also fully amphibious. The water propulsion is by hydro-jets, giving a speed of 8.5 km/h in the water.

Versions of the VAB currently being marketed are: an armoured personnel carrier for two crew plus ten fully equipped troops; an infantry fighting vehicle with a 12.7 mm or 25 mm gun; a Dragar turret; a command post vehicle; an anti-tank missile launcher turret; an 81 mm mortar carrier; a 320 mm heavy mortar tractor; an ambulance; a recovery vehicle fitted with a crane; an anti-riot vehicle; and a NBC reconnaissance vehicle.

## SPECIFICATION:

**Crew:** 2 + 10
**Armament:** 1 x 7.62 mm machine-gun
**Ammunition:** 3,000 rounds, 7.62 mm
**Dimensions:** length 5.9 m; width 2.5 m; height 2.1 m
**Weights:** combat 13,000 kg
**Engine:** Renault MIDS 06-20-45 diesel developing 220 hp
**Performance:** road speed 92 km/h; range 1,000 km; amphibious capability
**Armour:** all-welded hull provides protection from small-arms fire and shell splinters

# Vickers MBT Mk 1 Vijayanta and Mk 3

*The Vickers MBT Mk 3 is in service with the Kenyan and Nigerian armies*

**D**URING THE LATE 1950s THE Indian Government decided to set up a tank plant in India to meet the demands of the Indian Army. British and German MBT designs were compared and the balance came down in favour of the Vickers design in 1961. By 1963 the first prototypes were completed, one retained by Vickers, the other despatched to India. At the same time the factory was being developed at Avadi, near Madras, and the first locally made **Vickers MBT** rolled off the production line in 1969 (though it was largely made of UK-built components). Although production has now finished, over 2,200 of the **Vijayanta (Victorious)**, as it is known in Indian service, have been delivered to the Indian Army, with numbers of the MBT also being exported to Kuwait, Kenya and Nigeria.

The layout of the Vickers MBT is conventional, the driver at the front of the hull on the right, ammunition storage to the left, with the other three crew members in the turret. The engine and transmission are at the rear of the hull. The original engine and transmission were the same as the Chieftain MBT. However, in the late 1980s the Vijayanta was repowered using a Detroit Diesel 12v-71T turbo-charged 12-cylinder engine, which develops 720 hp.

The MBT is armed with an L7 series 105 mm tank gun, though the APFDS ammunition is manufactured locally. It also carries machine-guns coaxially and on the commander's cupola. Around 50 rounds of

105 mm ammunition is carried, along with over 3,000 rounds of 7.62 mm. The Vijayanta has also been successfully up-armoured using the locally made composite Kanchan system, developed by the Defence Metallurgical Research Laboratory at Hyderabad. A number of variants are believed to exist of the Vijayanta, including bridge-laying devices and self-propelled guns.

---

## SPECIFICATION:

**Vickers MBT Mk 1**
**Crew:** 4
**Armament:** 1 x 105 mm L7A2 rifled main gun, 1 x 12.7 mm Browning machine-gun ranging, 1 x 12.7 mm machine-gun anti-aircraft, 1 x 7.62 mm machine-gun coaxial
**Ammunition:** 50 rounds, 105 mm; 3,000 rounds, 7.62 mm
**Dimensions:** length 9.8 m; width 3.2 m; height 2.7 m
**Weight:** 39,000 kg (combat)
**Engine:** L60 Leyland Diesel developing 535 hp
**Performance:** road speed 50 km/h; range 530 km; fording capability 1.1 m
**Armour:** 80 mm composite armour

# Warrior APC/AIFV

**T**HE APCS OF THE 1960s, such as the British FV432 and US M113, were flexible, versatile platforms that still fulfil specialised roles today. They brought a level of mobility to the infantry that only tracked vehicles can, but they lacked the armour and firepower necessary to fight on the modern battlefield. At the end of the decade, therefore, the then Fighting Vehicles and Engineering Establishment at Chertsey began to study concepts for the next-generation vehicle: an infantry fighting vehicle with Chobham armour, a 30 mm Rarden cannon in a turret, and a 750 hp diesel engine. The tendering competition that ensued ended with the then GKN Sankey getting the nod to produce the Mechanised Combat Vehicle 80 (MCV-80) – but not before the US XM2 (which would become the M2 Bradley) had been studied.

The MCV-80 was designed to meet General Staff Requirement 3533, which looked for capacity for ten men (inc. driver and gunner); mobility to keep up with the Challenger; armour that could protect against indirect artillery fragments and direct machine-gun fire; and firepower for general support.

MCV-80 prototypes were ready for use in autumn 1984 exercises, and passed with flying colours, gaining for GKN the contract for the second and third batches, at that time a sizeable order of over 1,000 vehicles (it has been reduced by defence cuts). Given the name **Warrior** in 1985, production began in GKN's

*Warrior with appliqué armour on hull sides and front*

*The Warrior is armed with a 30 mm Rarden cannon*

Telford factory in 1986, the vehicle being declared operational in 1988.

While GKN was the prime contractor, the company only built the all-welded aluminium hull; Vickers built the turret, Perkins the power-plant, and many other companies produced subsystems. Final deliveries to the British Army were made in 1995, with a total of 789 vehicles – including command

*Warrior on exercise in Poland*

*Desert Warrior as supplied to the Kuwaiti Army*

vehicles (four versions), artillery observation vehicles (dummy Rarden cannon, six-man crew, battlefield surveillance radar, Marconi Battlefield Artillery Engagement System and EMI man-portable surveillance and target acquisition radar), FV513 recovery vehicles (five-man crew including three fitters; carries an earth anchor and winch to facilitate recovery; one-man turret armed with a 7.62 mm chain gun) and FV512 repair vehicles (similar to the FV513 but without the recovery equipment; can carry a Challenger power-pack on a trailer). The Warrior can also be adapted to missile armament – 105 Warriors received MILAN installations in preparation for the long-range TRIGAT ATGW – and can also be fitted with a Pearson mine plough or dozer blade. A desert variant was taken by Kuwait, who ordered just over 250 in 1994, the last ones reaching that country in 1997. While various other versions have been mooted, it has been decided that the Warrior will not see a mid-life upgrade but will be replaced by the FIFV (Future Infantry Fighting Vehicle) in the second decade of the twenty-first century.

The Warrior has proved to be everything that the British Army wanted, and performed effectively in the Gulf War. There and in Bosnia Warriors were fitted with passive armour on the sides and glacis: it proved effective against tank shells and an RPG7 but was incapable of stopping the damage done to the 3RRF Warriors destroyed in a 'blue-on-blue' or friendly fire engagement by USAF A-10 Thunderbolts.

## SPECIFICATION:

**Crew:** 3 + 7
**Armament:** 30 mm L21 Rarden cannon, 7.62 mm L94A1 coaxial chain gun, 8 x 66 mm smoke grenade dischargers
**Ammunition:** 250 rounds, main gun; 2,000 rounds, coaxial
**Dimensions:** length 6.34 m; height 2.735 m; width 3.034 m; ground clearance 0.49 m
**Weight:** empty 24,500 kg; loaded 28,000 kg
**Engine:** Perkins CV-8 TCA diesel of 550 hp
**Performance:** range 660 km; road speed 75mp/h; fording capability 1.3 m
**Armour:** n/a

# Wiesel 1 and 2: Light Tank/Recce Vehicle/Multi-purpose Carrier

M ANY YEARS AGO THE WEST GERMAN Army spotted the need for a light air-portable armoured tracked vehicle for use in the airborne brigades in a variety of roles. The result was the design development by Porsche in the early 1980s of the first **Wiesel**, the **Mark 1**, manufactured by MaK GmbH, which could come in two versions, armed with either TOW or a 20 mm cannon. Further turret and weapon systems were then tried as the Wiesel's versatility was exploited, with its capacity to fulfil attack, command, reconnaissance and support roles in rapid reaction forces

In 1984 the West German Army made an initial order of 312 vehicles. This order was later upgraded to 343, whilst the vehicle has also been demonstrated in Greece, Norway and Indonesia. The USA has also taken a number of demonstration models with a view to using them in robotic tank trials.

The main armament of the vehicle is either a 20 mm Rheinmetall cannon, which carries some 400 rounds of ammunition, or a Hughes TOW guided missile. Seven TOW missiles are carried, two of which are ready for use mounted in a dual pod on the turret.

*A Wiesel TOW (left) and Wiesel Mk 20 of the German Army advance at speed during an exercise*

The vehicle is powered by a standard VW production engine, which develops 87 hp. It is protected by an all-welded steel construction hull, which gives the crew a defence against 7.62 mm small-arms fire and shell splinters. The layout of the interior is standard, with the driver at the front with the engine to his left. The vehicle is very compact and light, and two can be carried by Sikorsky CH-53 aircraft and also slung underneath transport aircraft such as the C-160 and C-130.

## WIESEL 2

P ROTOTYPES OF THE **WIESEL 2** WERE delivered in 1994, featuring increased volume and capacity over the Mark 1 version (which is purely a weapons-carrying system) while retaining its air-portability. Thus the Mark 2 version has a stretched, deeper hull,

*Wiesel 1 (Tim Ripley)*

*Wiesel 2 (Tim Ripley)*

which enables it to be used more effectively as a multi-purpose carrier. It also features a new track configuration and a new power-pack featuring the Audi four-cylinder turbo-charged diesel engine developing 109 hp. The initial Mark 2 versions were armed with TOW ATGW or a KUKA turret mounting a Rheinmetall 20 mm 202 cannon, and had the capacity to carry a complement of infantry as well. Later loads range from Ozelot stinger missile pods in its anti-aircraft/air defence and anti-armour role to a six-man personnel carrier with a 7.62 mm machine-gun and the additional modification of a rear exit ramp door. As with many APCs, the Wiesel's versatility enables a wide spectrum of battlefield uses. There are also command and control, fire support, anti-aircraft, radar, ambulance, ammunition carrier, mortar, surveillance and reconnaissance and even remote-controlled robot variants.

## SPECIFICATION:

**Wiesel 1: Mk 20**
**Crew:** 2
**Armament:** 1 x 20 mm cannon
**Ammunition:** 400 rounds, 20 mm
**Dimensions:** length 3.3 m; width 1.8 m; height 1.9 m; ground clearance 0.30 m
**Weight:** empty 2,030 kg; combat 2,750 kg
**Engine:** VW 5-cylinder turbo-charged diesel developing 87 hp
**Performance:** road speed 80 km/h; range 780 km
**Armour:** all-welded steel hull offering protection against 7.62 mm

**Wiesel 1: TOW**
**Crew:** 3
**Armament:** Twin TOW ATGW pod
**Ammunition:** 7 x TOW
**Dimensions:** length 3.3 m; width 1.8 m; height 1.9 m; ground clearance 0.30 m
**Weight:** 2,800 kg
**Engine:** VW 5-cylinder turbo-charged diesel developing 87 hp
**Performance:** road speed 80 km/h; range 780 km
**Armour:** all-welded steel

**Wiesel 2: Multi-purpose carrier**
**Crew:** variant-dependent – up to 6
**Armament:** variant-dependent
**Dimensions:** length 6.28 m; width 2.55 m; height 2.45 m; ground clearance 0.30 m
**Weight:** 4,100 kg
**Engine:** Audi 4-cylinder turbo-charged diesel developing 109 hp
**Performance:** road speed 70 km/h; range 550 km
**Armour:** all-welded steel

# Glossary

| | |
|---|---|
| AAAV | Advanced Amphibious Assault Vehicle |
| AAV | Amphibious Assault Vehicle |
| ADATS | Air Defense Anti-Tank System |
| AEV | Armoured Engineer Vehicle |
| AIFV | Armoured Infantry Fighting Vehicle |
| AMX | *Atelier de Constuction d'Issy-les-Moulineaux* |
| AP | Armour Piercing |
| APC | Armoured Personnel Carrier |
| APFSDS | Armour Piercing Fin-Stabilised, Discarding Sabot |
| APHE | Armour Piercing High Explosive |
| AP-T | Armour Piercing – Tracer |
| ARRV | Armoured Repair and Recovery Vehicle |
| ARV | Armoured Recovery Vehicle |
| ASCOD | Austrian–Spanish Co-Operative Development |
| ASLAV | Australian Light Armoured Vehicle |
| ATGW | Anti-Tank Guided Weapon |
| AVLB | Armoured Vehicle Launched Bridge |
| AVRE | Armoured Vehicle Royal Engineers |
| CEV | Combat Engineer Vehicle |
| COTAC | *Conduite de Tir Automatique pour Char* |
| CRARRV | Challenger Armoured Repair and Recovery Vehicle |
| CSB | Close Support Bridge |
| CV | Combat Vehicle |
| CVRT | Combat Vehicle Reconnaissance Tracked |
| EAAK | Enhanced Appliqué Armor Kit |
| EOD | Explosive Ordnance Disposal |
| EPG | *Engin Principal du Génie* |
| ERA | Explosive Reactive Armour |
| FAR | *Force d'Action Rapide* |
| FIFV | Future Infantry Fighting Vehicle |
| FMC | Food Machinery Corporation |
| FV | Fighting Vehicle |
| GIAT | *Groupement Industriel des Armements Terrestres* |
| GCT | *Grande Cadence de Tir* |
| GTK | *Gepanzertes Transport-Kraftfahzeug* |
| HE | High Explosive |
| HEAT | High Explosive Anti-Tank |
| HEAT-FS | High Explosive Anti-Tank – Fin Stabilised |
| HE-FRAG | High Explosive – Fragmentation |
| HEI | High Explosive Incendiary |
| HEMAT | Heavy Expanded Mobility Ammunition Trailer |
| HESH | High Explosive Squash Head |
| HE-T | High Explosive – Tracer |
| HVM | High Velocity Missile |
| IFV | Infantry Fighting Vehicle |
| LAV | Light Assault Vehicle |
| LLLTV | Low Light Level Television |
| LPT | Low-Profile Turret |
| LVTP | Landing Vehicle Tracked Personnel |
| MBT | Main Battle Tank |
| MILAN | *Missile d'Infanterie Léger Anti-Char* |
| MLRS | Multiple Launch Rocket System |
| MPC | Multi-Purpose Carrier |
| MRAV | Multi-Role Armoured Vehicle |
| NBC | Nuclear, Biological and Chemical |
| PTG | *Poseur de Travures du Génie* |
| RISE | Reliability Improved Selected Equipment |
| SAM | Surface-to-Air Missile |
| SEP | Systems Enhancement Package |
| SLEP | Service Life Extension Program |
| SP | Self Propelled |
| SPAAG | Self-Propelled Anti-Aircraft Gun |
| TBT | Tank Bridge Transporter |
| TOW | Tube-Launched, Optically-Tracked, Wire-Guided |
| VAB | *Véhicule de l'Avant Blindé* |
| VBL | *Véhicule Blindé Léger* |
| VSEL | Vickers Shipbuilding and Engineering Ltd |

# Index